TRIGGERED

TRIGGERED

A Memoir of Obsessive-Compulsive Disorder

Fletcher Wortmann

Thomas Dunne Books
St. Martin's Press
New York

THOMAS DUNNE BOOKS.
An imprint of St. Martin's Press.

TRIGGERED: A MEMOIR OF OBSESSIVE-COMPULSIVE DISORDER. Copyright © 2012 by Fletcher Wortmann. All rights reserved. Printed in the United States of America. For information, address St. Martin's Press, 175 Fifth Avenue, New York, N.Y. 10010.

www.thomasdunnebooks.com
www.stmartins.com

ISBN 978-0-312-62210-7

First Edition: April 2012

P1

For other psychopaths; we souls that suffer

Contents

Acknowledgments

I'd like to thank William Carter, Robin Goldstein, the staff of the McLean Hospital OCD Institute, and especially Carol Hevia and Harold Kirby for their guidance through the long and uncomfortable treatment of my disorder.

I also want to thank my agent, Eric Lupfer, and my editor, Rob Kirkpatrick, for taking a gamble on an unproven author; and the Swarthmore College English Department, the Swarthmore *Phoenix,* and Professor Greg Frost, for accepting a highly unorthodox project and allowing the nascent version of *Triggered* to see publication.

ACKNOWLEDGMENTS

I need to thank David Russell, as well as the Center for Creative Youth, for helping me to understand what writing is, and what it can accomplish.

Finally, it should not come as a surprise to readers of this work that I am extraordinarily close to my family. But at the risk of sounding obsessive-compulsive, repeating it one last time can't hurt. My mother, my father, my sister, and our wonderful stupid animals: I could not have done this without you. Thank you. I love you, very much.

Do not call anything impure that God has made clean.
—Acts 10:15

Introduction

In June 2007 I was diagnosed with obsessive-compulsive disorder. Apart from this my life has been an agreeable one. I was raised in nondescript suburbia by a family that loved and provided for me. I have wanted for very little. Any troubles I endured were, as they say, only in my head.

OCD is an anxiety disorder. It's defined by a pathological intolerance of uncertainty, and by elaborate neutralizing rituals performed to eliminate this uncertainty. While counting and hand washing are the most visible manifestations of OCD, the disorder can assume a variety of forms. My own primary symptoms involve recurring intrusive thoughts, often containing extreme violent and sexual content. I also struggle with perfectionism, minor contamination issues, passivity (sometimes I can muster up some passive-aggression if I'm feeling saucy), scrupulosity (OCD plus Jesus), low self-esteem, and generalized social anxiety. While the symptoms of OCD are visible to the observer only in the most extreme circumstances, the disorder has influenced nearly every aspect of my thinking. I do not think that it is unreasonable to say that it has prevented me from actually living the first twenty years of my life.

Although I was not correctly diagnosed until recently, I began to see a psychologist when I was six. In high school I was misdiagnosed with depression and put on medication, which I took until the end of my freshman year at Swarthmore College. After I discontinued the medication, my symptoms began to escalate, exacerbated by academic stress and a Vicious-and-Spungen-level unhealthy relationship. In early July 2007 I had an emotional breakdown and was admitted to McLean Hospital. I subsequently spent the fall of 2007 in a residential program for obsessive-compulsives.

After returning to school I eventually published, pseudonymously, an early version of this material in the Swarthmore *Phoenix* as well as an excerpt under my name in the Swarthmore literary magazine *The Night Café*. The extensive revision that eventually produced this book has not been easy. Eight hundred words in a chapter is comfortable for an obsessive-compulsive, and sixteen hundred is manageable, but ten thousand is torture. Yet the project has not been without rewards. Freed of the limitations of its format, the thing hissed and fizzled, and expanded into an entirely new mode.

It is not perfect. Rude words and tacky references contaminate it. Yet, because I am confronting my OCD, I find this to be appropriate. I will not allow the disorder to sterilize my writing. I have told my story, as honestly as I can.

While I am unusual in that obsession has compromised and occasionally endangered my life, I believe that obsessive and compulsive tendencies are universal. Each of us attempts, at times, to live inside our mind. Each of us is vulnerable to the sick principle that we could, if only we thought long enough and hard enough, invent a way to compensate for the objective terrors of the world. We check lights, we wash hands, we plead forgiveness—not to be stronger or happier, but to be *certain*. And each time we do this we submit, a little, to a kind of living death. I have chronicled in exhaustive, embarrassing detail my own cognitive dysfunction in hopes that by understanding it I may better extract myself from its toxic influence. But if you recognize something of yourself in the qualities of my neurosis, please do not hesitate. Work against it. Find help if you need to.

1

Some Say the World Will End in Ice

And when the smoke cleared away, and I sought to look upon the earth, I beheld against the background of cold, humorous stars only the dying sun and the pale mournful planets searching for their sister.
—H. P. Lovecraft and Winifred V. Jackson, "The Crawling Chaos"

Unless you or someone close to you has been affected by obsessive-compulsive disorder, or you have taken a course in clinical psychology (I take great satisfaction in the fact that my school's psychology department no longer considers me "abnormal"), you probably know only the basics of OCD: superb personal hygiene, exceptional organizational skills, an inclination toward solving mysteries. For many, a number of alleged professionals in mental health issues among them, any understanding of the disorder ends here. Before I proceed I want to give a short explanation of OCD.

I regret to inform you that we have reached the "interactive" portion of the text. I'm going to propose a thought experiment. If it isn't too much trouble, I need you to look up. Do it. Now. No one's watching. Look around you. Study your surroundings. Now consider the possibility that, at any moment, the end of the world could occur. The ground cracks, the clouds spark with red lightning, hungry waters rise. The sky hums with annihilating angels. Feel free to incorporate details from your preferred apocalypse, as long as they fit the overall scenario. Imagine the final crisis of man. Let us pretend that the sky is falling.

Now I would like you to prove, with absolute certainty, that this is not true and that you are not about to be owned by God. Never mind if you are inside, or even in some kind of reinforced bunker, because for the purposes of argument the hypothetical bullet the universe has aimed at you will pierce any barrier. No rational force can protect you. You have literally moments to live, and you are wasting them reading a memoir.

Now, no one is saying that the world is definitely about to end. You could probably construct a strong argument that my impending doomsday is actually pretty unlikely. You could cite research studies, endless statistics, and I'm sure all of these would be very accurate and science-y. But you have to recognize that all of this goes only so far. You can present your evidence to me and I can ask, "How do you know that's right?" and then you can show me your citations and your annotated bibliography, but I can ask, "How do you know *that's* right?" I can ask this again and again, as many times as I need to. A 5 percent margin of error is all well and good but will be small comfort if you are the unlucky one in twenty around when shit gets real.

The truth is that you cannot prove anything one way or the other. Everything is possible. We live in a world not of certainty but of endless incalculable risk. The music of the spheres is chaos.

Now, before you panic, I'm going to suggest a possible resolution to this situation: The end of days will not occur until you close the covers of this book. You can postpone the apocalypse for as long as you like just by keeping the book open. The instant you shut it, however, everything will be destroyed. Again, I can't prove to you that this is the case, but considering that we aren't sure about the end of the world to begin with, I don't think this is unreasonable. I know it will be inconvenient to keep the book open, and I am sympathetic, but it's such a minor inconvenience considering what is at risk. Just keep it open, at least for a few more minutes. Then, when you get a chance, you can put it facedown on your desk and forget about it. Or you could nail it open to a plank of wood and hide it in the attic or something. It'll ruin the spine, sure, but that's a pretty minor sacrifice, considering you now hold in your hands the trigger to the extinction of all worlds.

But you tell me, "So what?" And you forget about the possibility of imminent destruction, and you go on with your day. May I congratulate you on your apparent sanity. I can continue the narrative, secure that your brain is functioning as advertised. But imagine that "so what" was not good enough. Imagine that you could not live happily without absolute certainty, and that it seemed reasonable for you to keep the book open as long as you could. In this case, certain additional preventative measures would be prudent.

Fortunately I just thought of some additional preventative measures. They won't make or break the deal, of course, but they'll help. Maybe. They shouldn't hurt, anyway. Listen: When you hit page one hundred, make sure you lick your finger before you turn the page. Actually, you'd better do that every ten pages. And when you do put the book down, make sure you shut the lights off before you leave the room—although it would probably be better if you flicked them twice first. Also, next time you're out, make sure to write down the remaining time on any parking meters you see. And you know what? I'm going to need you to count things. Like, red shoes or milk or something. Seriously, it doesn't really matter what. Just start counting shit. Like maybe you see three cars go by, just fucking one two three, like that. Just to be safe. Trust me, it'll help, maybe.

Of course none of these behaviors will definitely prevent the apocalypse, but they might protect you, and in these dire circumstances we need to do everything we can. These are inconveniences, but aren't they preferable to the end of the world?

No. Not really, unfortunately. It is possible for a human being to reach a point where incineration in divine fire would actually increase cognitive and behavioral functionality.

It does not end here. It cannot. Tell me: How do you know that you won't be killed by a falling meteor? How do you know that you shut off the toaster oven this morning? That one of the seething millions of bacteria on your hands will not kill you? That your friends don't all secretly hate you? Do you have religion? Do you have the *right* religion? Are you sure? Are you a pedophile, a necrophiliac, a rapist? A murderer? How can you know that these tendencies do not dwell latent inside you, waiting for the right moment to evince themselves in the most horrific manner possible? How do you know that you are not a monster? How do you know that it isn't the end of the world?

Everyone has moments when, against probability and common sense, we attempt to eradicate ordinary uncertainty using our minds. You get halfway around the block and then realize that you might have forgotten to lock the front door, so you drive back around to check it. It's near the end of the seventh inning and things aren't looking good, so you pull out your favorite baseball cap because sometimes it seems to help. You call your child's phone twice to make sure that she got to the party okay. You cross your fingers, you knock on wood, you wish on a coin or a star or a stray eyelash. Everyone does this. It's not a problem for most people.

OCD is called "the doubting disorder," at least among people inclined to give cutesy alliterative nicknames to mental illness. OCD is the pathological intolerance of risk, however minute, and the surrender to protective ritual, however unbearable. No matter how unlikely a feared consequence, if there exists even the fraction of a percent of a possibility that it could occur, the disorder is able to find purchase. It seeks out the cracks in our perception of reality, it finds the tiny darkened territories on our internal maps; and then ceaselessly, tirelessly, it sets about expanding them. These cartographic elaborations are careful and clever. You will not notice that anything has been changed until the ink starts to bleed through onto your hands, and then suddenly every inch of territory has been marked inaccessible. Everything is made unknown and unsafe. Here there be dragons.

OCD presents itself as an innocuous problem-solving

mechanism. If you have a problem, after all, you should try to find an answer. If there is danger, you should protect yourself. So when you are confronted with the possibility of an undesirable occurrence, the disorder suggests modes of defense. Its voice is like that of a beloved grandmother, recently passed away and resurrected by evil ritual. It is maternal, condescending, and affectionate, with a slight suggestion of righteous indignation. "I know what's best for you, dear," it says, a hint of formaldehyde on its breath, a tiny fly crawling on its unblinking painted eye. You listen, compelled by guilt and fear, despite the suspicion that this cannot end well.

The disorder promises what it does not have the power to give. As you accept its reasoning, as you begin to work with it, it tightens its hold on you. It exaggerates danger and then offers a modicum of relief through an ever-expanding web of regulation and restriction. OCD insinuates itself delicately until you are utterly constrained, until every moment of existence is a choice between submission to the rule of an absurd tyrant and absolute terror. Eventually the behavior of the sufferer is entirely divorced from reality. Hand washing is no longer a basic hygienic practice but a magic charm, a banishment cast against the immaterial, malevolent threat of "germs." Strange trigonometries are calculated and then arbitrarily discarded at the disorder's whim. The world is perceived through a fine mesh of obsession. Everything is connected; everything shines like a razor with terrible significance.

OCD demands safety and certainty, and the fact that nothing can ever really be proven is regrettable but irrelevant to its purposes. It is the anti-life equation, and it will demonstrate to you, if you allow it, that free will is illusory and that everything wants you dead. It wants life to become a chessboard and then for all of the black squares to be systematically removed. It wants the world to be as small as a room and then small as your head and then even smaller than that. I did any number of asinine, irrational things not because they *would* protect me, but because I thought they *might,* and I'd be damned if the one night I failed to properly pray the Lord my soul to keep was the night I died before I woke.

Only recently have I recognized how intrinsically fucked my childhood psychology was. My earliest years were relatively free of this mental constipation. I was born in Winchester, Massachusetts, a thoroughly adequate suburb of Boston. My parents got together some time after college. As they later explained to me, they found my name in one of those baby books while driving. "That's it!" my mother cried out in jubilation when she discovered it between "Fleming" and "Flint," presumably causing my surprised father to swerve the car in a manner inadvisable for his pregnant passenger, and ensuring that I would suffer ridicule from my peers for the next decade and a half.

My mother grew up in a home of prodigious achievers; her father ran the local Boys & Girls Club, accepting responsibility for an entire town full of wayward children. Because of this she grew up with constant constructive criticism from her parents. Her father, as she occasionally reminded me, would check her freshly made bed once a week and force her to remake it if he could not bounce a dime off the perfectly stretched-out sheets. As a result, my mother was often strict with me, sometimes unreasonably although never maliciously. Antiquated terms such as *persnickety* or *flibbertigibbet* are perhaps appropriate. My mother has a very goofy sense of humor and remains prone to making comments and suggestions so absurd that they demonstrate either a complete disconnect from reality or a desire to drive her children mad. As a child I was unable to leave the house each morning without her asking at least three times, in a little singsong chant, if I had remembered my lunch box. After I sneezed loudly in high school she once asked me, in the car pool and in front of my peers, what color my mucus was. It was irritating and endearing in equal measure. Her rigidity was always cut with whimsy.

My father came from a home constantly on the verge of fracture, though never quite breaking. You would never suspect this, to speak with him. He is easygoing, friendly, occasionally oblivious, and has a fondness for dumb jokes. But he grew up neglected, his own parents afflicted by depression, abuse, and alcoholism. I never knew either of my father's parents, really, although I was very much a product of their genetic legacy. The cocktail mixed from my parents' strains, these polar tendencies toward perfectionism and despair, would prove toxic.

My parents were good to me. Sometimes they were stern, but just as often they were kind and understanding. Under ordinary circumstances I would have no reason to fault them for my upbringing, but through the lens of my illness they appeared as strange heathen idols, distant and unyielding. Together, quite unintentionally, they nurtured the disorder. I learned from them to self-punish, to endure absurd trial. My father would work late into the night for his firm and for the town conservation commission, but it was really my mother who impressed upon me the obsessive-compulsive habits of highly effective people. One morning, for example, while locking my sister and me into the car, she accidentally banged her head against the door, suffering a sizable gash. Rather than seek immediate medical assistance, she chose to take my sister and me to school first, endangering herself and her children, the trickle of blood into her eyes obstructing her vision and driving her closer to unconsciousness. Later she would cite this incident as an example of endurance and fortitude in the face of crisis. My mother had a habit we referred to with begrudging affection as her "off-offs": before each family vacation she would return to the house one last time to ensure that no stray appliance had been left on. She was also responsible, she informed us, for the foundation of a Ban the Beatles from Boston society as a schoolgirl in the early 1960s; despite its catchy name, B3 somehow reveals itself to be lamer and lamer each time I remember it.

I took careful notes on her meticulousness and her occasional moral panic, as did the disorder. It would gorge itself on my parents' love and affection just as it did on their mistakes. Any reprimand or praise they gave me was multiplied a thousandfold in my mind, internalized and inflicted again and again. Of course, I cannot blame my mother and father for this any more than I can blame myself. If I criticize my parents in these pages, it is not out of malice or bitterness, but from a need to relate the psychological circumstances of my childhood as accurately as I can. Considering how vulnerable I was, it was inevitable that any parent, no matter how sensitive, would wreak psychic havoc on me. They loved me, and they did as well as they could under profoundly difficult conditions.

My younger sister was born two years after I was, and I was first introduced to her as a bespectacled, babbling thing. We got along pretty well. Later, when my friends complained of knockdown fights and drunken shouting matches with their siblings, I was always baffled. My sister and I did not fight, usually, and when we did it was followed by immediate guilt and then reconciliatory hugging. I love my sister, and it seems that the best way for me to express my affection in this book is to leave her out of it as much as possible. Again, I would have had no reason to complain about our relationship had the OCD not been present to exploit it. I loved her, and for the disorder this meant she was Something Important That Could Be Hurt.

But that was much, much later. For about half a decade, my mind seemed functional, and my memories of early childhood are fond if indistinct. I made friends and I developed elaborate backstories for my stuffed toys. Through a freak accident of child-care administration I became the oldest student in my kindergarten class—not necessarily something to be proud of in high school or college, but at the time it seemed pretty sweet. Most vividly I remember my mother, each morning during our ride to school, entertaining my sister and me with improvised stories. We demanded that she invent further adventures for our favorite cartoon characters, and she acquiesced, and soon the three of us had developed an instant-oatmeal oral tradition, a sprawling fan-fiction mythology that spanned the width and depth of children's media. My sister and I enjoyed this tremendously, and despite constant demands on her creative faculties, I think that our mother did, too.

I started first grade at a local public school, where I lasted about four months. My parents tell me that I outpaced the curriculum, that I wasn't being offered sufficient academic challenge; my primary memories of this time are of terror and boredom and wishing that I could go and do the whole kindergarten thing over again. Partway through the year, I was informed that I would be plucked from my local public school and transplanted into the flowering educational hothouse of a "progressive" private school in Watertown. Here I would call my teachers by their first names, and would be strongly encouraged to compose interpretive poetry about clouds instead of learning long division. This all sort of made sense at the time.

Unfortunately, I had difficulty making friends in this new environment. Loneliness would be something of a recurring motif throughout my otherwise happy childhood. I may have been the big-kid badass in kindergarten, when an inclusive birthday party and a convincing fake belch were the only prerequisites for popularity, but after that I often found myself alone. As the disorder began to develop, I experienced greater difficulty allowing myself to make friends. How could I not, when even the mildest suggestion of disapproval from a peer became a scathing insult? The OCD could pick out an overheard comment or a hostile impression and then use it to convince me that I was universally despised. If I did not have proof that I was loved, then I thought I must have been hated. I was so terrified of social rejection, of the scorn and mockery of my peers, that I began a preemptive campaign of comprehensive self-criticism to protect myself from their judgment. Rather than risk isolation, I shut myself down entirely and so ensured it. If I told a joke, it was carefully scripted, rehearsed countless times in my head before I could take a chance repeating it out loud. I would not allow a single word to pass my lips unless I could convince myself, with scientific rigor, that my discourse was irrefutably awesome. I am told, by those who knew me, that I was a quiet child.

(Oddly enough, one of my classmates also had OCD, although he was fortunate enough to find a therapist who recognized it early on. His name was Gus: he was a counter and a cleaner and so was quickly diagnosed. I feel about Gus now the way a young child might feel about a baby sister or brother who arrives and suddenly wins all of the parents' attention and is showered with gifts and surprises. His symptoms were quickly identified. He published a little picture book about OCD for kids, and he went on a nationally televised talk show and everyone told him how brave and special he was. My resentment is petty and bratty and basically entirely unjustified, but still: The kid scratched off most of my life's ambitions by age ten, more or less by accident.)

My social paralysis did not, at least, interfere with my class work. Insomuch as we were actually graded at the progressive elementary school I did well, and the squares I received far outnumbered the circles and X's. But recess, instead of a daily break, became a period of unique and quiet unhappiness. For one half hour a day I was necessarily silent, and thus alone. I found ways of passing the time, of course, by counting pebbles on the playground or building makeshift toys from bits of garbage. Occasionally my desperation led me to play with the younger children, my acceptance predetermined by my advanced age and my presumably sophisticated vocabulary of swear words. But just as often I was alone.

I remember once in fifth grade, on a particularly grim and rainy afternoon on the verge of breaking into downpour, I demanded that recess be canceled so that I could stay inside and use the computer. This would be just as solitary but probably more entertaining. When my demands were not met I still refused to leave the classroom, and rather than submit and play outside with the other students, I let myself be taken to the principal's office. I accepted this punishment with unwarranted self-righteousness, like a political dissident persecuted for my beliefs. Yet I was not the only prisoner taken that day by these innovative and sympathetic fascist educators. In the office, I found an equally frustrated sixth grader whose class was instructed to remain inside and work instead of playing in the rain. He amused himself by making paper planes and subversively wrote on the side of one that at our school "you can't go to hell because you're already in hell." I grinned politely, as if there were a joke to get. Even as a child, the absurdity of this situation did not escape me.

Another time I became so caught up in a geometry problem before recess that I accidentally stayed inside, working, through the duration of the period. When I tired of studying I demanded to be compensated for my "overtime," and my instructors agreed and took me outside. It was winter, and several days after a heavy snow, so the school grounds were covered with a thin sheet of ice that I could just stomp through if I tried. I spent the period alone on a field of uninterrupted white beneath a cloudless sky, punching out shards of ice and piling them into towers and castles. Our school grounds were not large, but in the shining contrast of unbroken white and blue they seemed almost infinite. Throughout my life I would suffer countless episodes of torment at the hands of my disorder, but I cannot recall ever feeling quite as lonely as I did that afternoon.

Things were better at home. When I was very young my family owned a miscellany of elderly cats, each of which I remember positively but without much affection, but around third grade my mother decided to indulge us by purchasing a family dog. One night she coyly informed us that we would be driving out to pick up a friend of my father's, and we drove to an out-of-state breeder to find that our mysterious guest would not be a smelly middle-aged lawyer, as we'd expected, but an adorable black Labrador puppy. Our exhilaration was short-lived, however, for soon after we began the ride home poor little Bear (as we named him) suddenly realized the implications of his rapidly shifting fortunes and began to wail like a banshee. "Take him back!" I shouted, convinced the little screaming thing was defective. "Take him back!"

In retrospect I am grateful my parents did not heed my demands. Our family would have been poorer for it. Bear was a champion dog: loyal, affectionate, and alternately gentle or ferocious or joyous as the situation demanded. He was also incredibly stupid. Indeed, his certification as a pedigree-bred black Lab was the only way to explain his epic imbecility because frankly there is no way his ancestors could have survived in the wild. You could take his bowl of supper, lift it to your mouth, and make scarfing noises, and this would send him into fits. Or you could fill his water dish with seltzer and he would drink it and then spit it out, scowling, only to return a few moments later to drink from it again, apparently having forgotten the whole ordeal. If you convincingly mimicked a throwing motion during a game of fetch without actually releasing the ball, Bear would tear out after the imaginary ball and then look back, dumbfounded, incapable of comprehending your betrayal. And when you did throw the ball, there was always a chance that he would chase it headfirst into a tree.

A few months later, after some consideration, my parents informed me that I would be allowed to have a pet of my own, provided it did not tear open the garbage or incite random barking fits in the middle of the night. Although I was sorely tempted by the horrible, hideous leopard gecko, I eventually relented to my mother's suggestions and picked a kitten from a local animal shelter. He was a soft, pliable thing, a Ragdoll Siamese mix. I called him Moonbeam, the "moon" in reference to his cream-white fur and the "beam" to his electric blue eyes; the name evoked for me images of occult mystery, the bright concentration of lunar energies, and I thought that it sounded pretty badass. I was wrong, of course, but no amount of gentle parental suggestion could persuade me of this. Anyway the name fit for a little while, for the month or so before he began to grow. Then it became inappropriate, and then embarrassing, and then hilarious, and then somehow improbably it circled back around to fitting him perfectly.

I was a very sensitive child. As I grew I remained soft, for quite a while, until undesirable circumstances forced me to change. As Moonbeam grew he also remained soft, but he compensated for the constant of his pillowy density with an ever-expanding variable diameter. He grew dark and enormous, his coat more coffee than cream and sagging around his thighs and gut. The bright, sweet kitten disappeared, assimilated into mounds of doughy flesh. When he sat down, it was a collapse, a sudden deliberate collision, the sheer force of it audible even through his layers of padding. Only the eyes remained the same, still sparkling with wicked intelligence.

As he grew older, Moonbeam began to play games with us, some gentle and others cruel and psychological. He splayed himself out over household appliances, he threw down his weight in undesirable places—on newspapers or fresh linen, in bathtubs. He had a remarkable habit of materializing on a stair an instant before you could step on it, forcing you to maneuver quickly in order to avoid him. He fetched and carried small objects and toys. He might approach a book or a glass of water and then nudge it gently toward the edge of the table, send it tumbling, and then stare at you, mocking and indifferent. His games were never for his own amusement. They were a means to an end. He wanted our attention, demanded it, and it did not matter to him whether it was won through affection or aggravation.

It has been suggested that the opposite of love is not hatred but apathy. While I am not sure if a human being is capable of positively expressing disdain or indifference, I am certain that Moony could. There is nothing so utterly dismissive as the "fuck off" of a cat. It is untempered by compassion or restraint. When he wanted to, Moonbeam could be utterly apathetic, so disdainful that he would actually still suffer you to stroke him and utter endearments, your presence so loathsome as to be beneath his contempt. If you held him he would squirm until free. Restriction was offensive to him. If you left the front door open and unattended for even a second he would bolt outside, and then after hours of calling and crying and printing lost-cat posters, you would watch him saunter up as if nothing had happened. If you locked him in a room he would search every crevice for means of escape, and failing this he'd shit in a corner to demonstrate his displeasure.

He was a bastard animal. His affection could never be demanded, only freely given. But he could perceive pain the way he could hear the sound of dry kibble poured into a dish from across the house, and he was generous to his companions in our moments of unhappiness. He would climb in uncomfortable places, gently head–butt your shoulder. He would roll at your feet so suddenly and enthusiastically as to threaten to trip you. He would swat at you or sit up and stare and mew, once, with considerate restraint. He was kind, but in his kindness he demonstrated lunacy and joy. In these moments he was absurd but never cruel, gentle but never maudlin. He would comfort you and, in the same moment, remind you of the absurdity of your sorrow. This was his greatest trick, more than fetching rubber balls or mysteriously pressing through seemingly tightly shut doors.

I loved Bear and Moonbeam in different ways suitable to their natures. Bear was a dog, and although I was not our family's alpha (it was my father he regarded with unwavering, slobbering devotion), I was a brother, another member of his pack. We would run and wrestle, and he was oddly undismayed if I kicked him in the face. I loved Bear like a dog. I loved him for his devotion and idiocy and for the immeasurable joy he snatched from every instant of his life.

Moonbeam was a more complicated creature. He was capricious. He snarked and teased. But despite his reflexive hostility toward restraint, he was an incredibly affectionate animal. I loved him like a cat, sitting with him in silence when he allowed it, propping him up on his hind legs and forcing him to do little dances when he did not. The animals would do much to distract me from my condition. They were kind to me when I was sick.

While my family and animals helped me retain my sanity, other powers conspired to undermine it. A significant barrier to my social acclimation was that I lived beneath a dangling sword of soul-obliterating guilt. I understand that Irish-Catholics have something of a reputation for self-recrimination, but I took special pride in the absolute cruelty I inflicted on myself. Anything even slightly objectionable that I did, or even saw, would trouble my soul until I confessed it to a proper authority. I could not hear a classmate cuss without feeling the overwhelming urge to cleanse my tainted thoughts. (These were not mind-blowing swears, either. A "butt" or a "fart" or even a meager "shut up," without any scatological implications, was enough to send me into fits of self-flagellation.) Sometimes I would confess to a teacher or a priest, but most often for reasons of convenience I sought clemency from my mother. She became a figure of divine forgiveness, dispensing absolution with a single shrug or eye roll. School was a silent moral vigil, as I was burdened with a growing litany of imagined transgressions over the course of each day. Each afternoon when my mother picked me up she would ask me how school had been, and each afternoon she suffered through a torrent of impure thoughts, overheard oaths, and unacted violent urges before any actual information was exchanged. I would convey to her my daily confession of entirely forgivable sins, and she would absolve me with a murmur of "that's dumb" or "don't worry about it."

(It should be noted that I was not the only member of my family afflicted by crippling guilt. Bear, in his youth, was a prodigious consumer of forbidden foodstuffs: garbage, a pie, or stick of butter left unattended on the counter. Once I came home from a classmate's birthday triumphant, having kicked royal ass against the piñata, but when I awoke the next morning I found only a few scraps of candy wrapper remained of my spoils. Once Bear ate crayons and shat rainbow for a week. In each of these cases, he was visibly overwhelmed by guilt. Each time we discovered evidence of one of his crimes, Bear would inevitably be found cowering only a short distance away, paralyzed by shame and indigestion, his tail wagging nervously and his body jerking away from the mildest scold as if struck. We all had a good laugh whenever this happened, and Bear inevitably got off without much of a punishment, so in retrospect he may have benefited from his expression of atonement. Not that I think he feigned remorse to soften us up. He was far too honest and far, far too stupid for this.)

While obsession was sometimes blunt and cruel, at other times its influence was subtler. When I was very young, I became fascinated with dinosaurs. I understand such preoccupations are not unusual among young gentlemen of a certain age, but my enthusiasm was beyond anything reasonable. I memorized facts and figures, Latin names. I read every book in the library—even the ones from the seventies, which showed sauropods wading in suspiciously deep swamps and tyrannosaurs upright and pudgy like monstrous file clerks, just so that I could revel in how outdated the illustrations were. I saw dinosaurs everywhere—in clouds and trees, in bits of trash. It was as if these animals were deliberately created, by evolution or by an intelligent but petty designer, to captivate me. They were huge and powerful, but they were classifiable, and I could master and control them with my mind.

My obsession with dinosaurs became the model for a recurring pattern of consumption as I grew. Every year or two, I would find some new subject or corporate intellectual property and devote myself utterly to its study: floppy bean-bag animals that I adored and then remorselessly shoved into my closet, a sixteen-bit videogame series that I would never actually touch outside of brief tantalizing moments at toy store console displays. I flirted with *Star Wars*, but ultimately preferred the Wagnerian-but-with-robots Sturm und Drang of Hasbro's Transformers. I collected the physical objects associated with the franchise—videos, toys, chintzy fast-food promotional giveaways that did not "transform" so much as "hinge" or "sit immobile"—but these were never the point. These were relics, graven images, important only in that they allowed access to a profound state of being. It was the collection in my head that mattered. It was like having a wonderful toy box in my mind, full of objects that I could take out and play with whenever I was bored or sad or hurt.

My parents were deeply ambivalent about my consumption of this pop-culture junk. My mother was supreme judge of all entertainment, and guilt prevented me from enjoying any book or television program I knew she might disapprove of. I remember once when I was thirteen, my father offered to take me to *The Matrix*. Although he had reviewed the film and determined that it was appropriate, I could not be content without endorsement from both parents. "Wow," I said a little too eagerly, desperately hoping my mother would overhear my cleverly veiled confession. "My first R-rated movie!" She heard it. "John," she said to my father, "it doesn't have any . . . boy-girl stuff, does it?" A short quarrel followed, and my mother confirmed my suspicions that the film would seriously unhinge me. Such exchanges were common. My mother recognized I was oversensitive, and throughout my childhood she risked overprotecting me. I cannot blame her.

My father's concerns were not psychological but practical. He encouraged me to save my allowance instead of spending it, and referred to the toys as "unnecessary plastic objects." This was anathema to me. It was agony. The idea that I could do something to displease my parents, the people whom I loved most in the world and whom I had to obey at all costs, was excruciating. I was addicted, and I knew this and I was profoundly ashamed of it. It was not enough that I was obsessed with Transformers. I was *tormented* in my obsession with Transformers, I was filled with guilt and forbidden longings about plastic robots. Several times I tossed the things from my room in a pile, consumed by self-loathing and rage, only to scoop them back up to my bosom later like a junkie.

At other times my parents seemed perfectly happy to use my fixations as an unnecessary plastic carrot to encourage good behavior. Around the time I was in third and fourth grade my mother served on a town volunteer committee. During meetings my sister and I would be left in the town hall with a book or a homework assignment, asked to busy ourselves and stay quiet. I thus developed a deep Pavlovian reaction to certain back rooms in old buildings, to ugly houndstooth rugs and stacked plastic chairs, to the hum of fluorescent lighting punctuated by a ticking clock. These things still summon for me feelings of isolation and anticipation. When we were good (and we learned very quickly to be good) sometimes my mother would take us out to buy a toy afterward. I believe that this practice had a profound influence on my moral development. Being good meant being quiet, and obedient. Suffering, especially pointless suffering, was rewarded. I remember as a child pining for these moments, looking for new ways to be hurt and abandoned. I sought out pain so that I could survive it and be rewarded.

While unmistakable in retrospect, at the time my symptoms resisted easy diagnosis. They transmuted, slipping through the fingers like quicksilver. Many of my early obsessions fixed not on illness or uncleanliness but on imminent apocalypse. In first grade, an overzealous classmate claimed that countless generations from now our sun would overheat and explode; the same year a visiting musical environmental group made the (retrospectively somewhat dubious) claim that given our current rate of deforestation, the Earth would *run out of oxygen* by 2005. I spent weeks paralyzed by dread, arguing against the possibility of these hypothetical apocalypses. I tirelessly debated with myself, determined to prove that these scenarios could never occur, never quite succeeding.

But my first full-blown bout with OCD I owe to Kurt Vonnegut. My third-grade teacher, thoughtlessly neglecting the handful of her charges suffering from undiagnosed madness, told us about a book she was reading. That book was Vonnegut's *Cat's Cradle*. In her

predigested version of the novel, the world was threatened by the evil molecule Ice-9, which would supposedly freeze every nonwater substance on the planet once
released. I imagine that Kathleen (we called her Kathleen, never Mrs. or Ms., as we drew pictures of sym-
phonies and continued not learning long division) had
forgotten this by the end of the day. I imagine the other
students forgot it, too.

But oh Lordy, I did not forget it. I could not forget
it, no matter how hard I tried. The threat of Ice-9 was
real to me, even though I understood that the actual
substance of Ice-9 was emphatically not; if some hack
sci-fi writer had imagined the stuff, then surely it could
be re-created in reality. More to the point, could I ever
prove to myself that it couldn't be? Ice-9 consumed my
days, it suffused into my schoolwork and my dreams.
The threat of Ice-9 could not be eradicated, no matter
how many times my parents assured me that the stuff
did not exist, no matter how many times my therapist
had me write its name on a scrap of lined paper and
burn it or tear it or flush it down the toilet. My only
strategic recourse, the only thing I could do, was to
spend every waking moment examining my surroundings and considering my course of action, should the
hypothetical cryopocalypse occur. I spent hours studying the position of sinks and flow of water from leaky
fountains, planning how I would contact my parents

and gather supplies in the frozen wasteland. No matter where I went or what I did, I was haunted by an invisible wave of cold blue, driving forward, uncontrollable and unstoppable because it did not exist. I bathed ice and showered ice, I slept, drank, and breathed it. My brain seized up and solidified, tattooed by frost, a cool blue chemical pearl.

What eventually saved me was my father. After I'd suffered several months of crippling anxiety and fruitless counseling, my father offhandedly mentioned that I'd had it wrong the whole time. Fans of Vonnegut will have seen this coming: In the novel Ice-9 didn't freeze everything *except* water. It froze *only* water. And suddenly, just like that, the paralysis was shattered. Of course! Triumph! The imaginary freezing molecule I dreaded was only *made up,* completely different from the imaginary freezing molecule that actually imaginarily existed! *Ice-9 froze only water! Of course!* It was all a big misunderstanding. My family and I could certainly survive that kind of chemical doomsday. We'd cross the frozen oceans and hunt penguins. No big deal. Problem solved. The reasoning behind the whole process was aggressively nonsensical, of course, and could be dismissed easily by any sane individual. "Why didn't you just stop worrying about it earlier?" I can hear you ask, and my only response is that I was psychologically incapable of doing so. I am not sane. I wish I could offer a more satisfying narrative explanation, with character development and such, but for what it's worth, the whole mess never made much sense to me, either. This is why we call it a disorder.

It was in this moment of release that my OCD seduced me. This was the moment when everything it had promised me finally came true. This is how the disorder perpetuates itself: by occasionally rewarding trauma and neurosis with brief moments of relief. Every so often, everything will work, and you will somehow convince yourself that you are safe,. and the disorder will claim credit. With Ice-9 I had encountered a scenario that caused me tremendous anxiety; I writhed and fixated, obsessed, for several months, trying to discover a way to disprove it; and then finally, finally, I learned an arbitrary piece of information I had previously overlooked that somehow eliminated my anxiety entirely. The fact that the obsession and my eventual relief were not related in any way, by cause or effect, never occurred to me. I had struck a bargain with the OCD, and after long months of struggle the disorder seemed to fulfill its promise. The transaction was complete. In that moment I became subservient to it.

2

Every Day Is Like Sunday

To bring disquietude and disturbance on a soul when it is praying, or trying to pray, he endeavors to excite impure feelings in the sensory part. And if people pay attention to these, the devil does them great harm. . . .

And that is not all; for to make them cowardly and afraid, he brings vividly to their minds foul and impure thoughts. And sometimes the thoughts will concern spiritual things and persons who have been a help to them. Those who attribute any importance to such thoughts, therefore, do not even dare look at anything or think about anything lest they thereupon stumble into them.

These impure thoughts so affect people who are afflicted with melancholia that one should have great pity for them; indeed, these people suffer a sad life.

—Saint John of the Cross, commentary on "Dark Night"

I have found Catholicism and obsessive-compulsive disorder to be deeply sympathetic to each other. One is a repressive construct founded in existential terror, barely restrained by complex, arbitrary ritual behaviors; the other is an anxiety disorder. As such, the irrational anxiety born of mental illness and the healthy, spiritually redemptive anxiety prescribed by a millennia-old patriarchy are almost indistinguishable from each other. The teachings of the Catholic Church were hugely influential on the development of my neuroses. Catholicism established a useful context of guilt and self-loathing that the disorder could exploit.

Although I grew up a strict Catholic, my family did not raise me that way. Because of my father's lax Protestant upbringing, my mother decided that every Sunday my sister and I would be bundled up in something presentable and dragged to St. Eulalia's in Winchester. I cannot remember my first time in church, presumably because I was too busy napping or vomiting on something consecrated to pay attention. As I had been brought up on cartoons and videogames, my patience for spiritual matters was limited. I might have been able to work up some interest in the Garden of Eden, with its cute animals and gratuitous nudity, but anything else was beyond me. Our mother decided, given our short attention spans, that during Mass my sister and I would be sequestered with the other young children in the balcony at the back of the church.

This was, as a carved wooden sign warned: A PLACE TO PRAY, NOT A PLACE TO PLAY. My mother wisely disregarded this. So my sister and I were given little note-books to draw in, and on Christmas we were allowed to bring toys, and so like any good American Catholic I developed a Pavlovian association between Jesus Christ and plastic transforming dinosaurs. This association was reinforced at my first Holy Communion, when I received a Nerf foam-ball bazooka. Thoughtfully, my parents forbade me from aiming the gift at anyone's face, reinforcing both the Christian value of nonviolence and also the tactical importance of groin damage. The con-sequence of this was that, as a child, I came to associate the Catholic Church with two things: new toys and bore-dom. The sight of a crucifix would send my devout little hands a-twitching with material lust.

Eventually, however, I started to pay attention to what was being said in Mass, and the words of the father brought me to a profound and uniquely religious state. I became confused. The whole Genesis business, for example, seemed to unravel the more I thought about it. The world created in seven days, the woman produced from the body of the man, the complete, disappointing absence of any dinosaurs: There was no way the church could expect me to accept this sort of thing at face value. I mean, they said that there were no dinosaurs, for Christ's sake. There were occasional concessions made—there was even a picture in my children's Bible of an obese brachiosaur trudging around the Edenic swamp—but the church seemed more comfortable brushing the whole issue under the rug. How, metaphorically or literally, could you brush a brachiosaur under the rug? The church's dismissal of modern science upset me. I was finished, I decided, with religion and its unenlightened, dinosaur-denying ways.

But if I was done with Catholicism my mother was not, and I was drafted into CCD, the church's afterschool education program. It was here that I was convinced of the grave error of my heretical, dinosaur-loving beliefs. Catholicism, it turned out, was pretty serious stuff. This God fellow was not to be messed with. God was always watching us, and God was judgmental and full of wrath, and God had *very* particular ideas about what one could and could not do with one's genitals. To cross God meant dire consequences. Because if God was sufficiently angry with you and your vile, sinful genitals, you could wind up in hell.

Of course, hell was never explained in any great detail, but between the ominous hints given by my CCD teacher and my own investigations I had a pretty clear picture of what went on there. Hell was terrible. It was always nighttime in hell, and you never got any pizza or ice cream, and you were sodomized by the demon-king Mammon, your innards turned to slag by his six throbbing members and ejaculate of molten rock. You couldn't go swimming or ride your bike, and everyone wanted to hurt you. Santa Claus never visited hell, and for Christmas your presents were delivered by a six-headed cow fetus with a screaming razor-toothed mouth instead of udders. And your presents were all eyeballs. Hell was a bad place, I decided, and I didn't want to go there. It was a simple matter of cost-benefit analysis. I could be pious and presumably miserable for my eighty years on Earth and guarantee my place in paradise, or I could enjoy myself now and then spend eternity having my intestines gnawed on by eel-eyed demon-whores made from human entrails. I would be stupid not to make the long-term investment.

And hell was inescapable, in the sense that everywhere you found people who wanted to tell about it: not just in Mass, but on billboards and bumper stickers, and on the weird cable channels with cheap-looking puppets. I endured unprovoked evangelism from wild-eyed homeless men and stone-faced proselytizing at the feet of yarn-haired sock prophets. I was bombarded with Jack Chick comics, in which nebbish evangelicals quarrel with demons for the souls of agnostic morons; in one the devil discredits the fundamentalist's literature by proclaiming, "I *don't* want you to read this propaganda, kid—it'll make you mentally sick!"

As a small child, I had yet to develop the veneer of misanthropy and cynicism that would protect me in my later years. I made the mistake of being innocent, credulous, prone to wonder. I was easily swooned by sparkle or hellfire. Evangelical material like this stands against humanity, against life, and in favor of suffocating dogma. It is corrosive. It burns and then sterilizes, and it is produced and distributed with the explicit intent of exploiting those who are vulnerable. If this material did not align itself with the ideological bedrock of Western civilization, I imagine it would be condemned by the very people who promote it. I am not one to advocate censorship, but still: Won't someone think of the children?

In retrospect, what baffles me about the concept of hell is this. In hell, I was told, God will inflict pain on you. For all of the impassioned language and nightmare imagery, that is all that hell means. There is always some reference to guilt, yes, to repentance, as the name of the Lord turns to hot lead in the mouths of the rueful damned. But this is secondary. You will try to repent only because God is torturing you, but God will not stop torturing you. God will hurt you. He will keep hurting you. Two thousand years of theological debate, and this is their ultimate punishment, this is the scariest thing these cocksuckers could come up with. Boring, ordinary, physical pain. Hell is putting your hand on a hot stove for the rest of eternity. Hell is the worst stubbed toe of all time. Don't misbehave or you'll get a spanking. More than anything else, this now strikes me as profoundly unimaginative.

As I was tutored in the wages of sin during CCD, I also practiced the economics of redemption. We watched a movie about a historical manifestation of the Virgin Mary in Portugal, which my Google-fu suggests was the 1952 film *The Miracle of Our Lady of Fatima*. The film was quite goofy and should by all means be pursued by connoisseurs of awkwardly earnest religious cheese. But Catholicism doesn't do camp. The film was produced and presented to us with aching sincerity. What I remember most clearly was a scene in which a child actor asks the shiny cellulose acetate Virgin Mary what has happened to her recently deceased friend. The little girl's friend, the Virgin Mary sweetly explains, is in purgatory. That broke my brain a little. The girl in the film was only six or seven at the most, and her friend must have been even younger when she died. What did the little girl do, in five years of brief life, to disqualify her from salvation? Was the little Portuguese girl smoking and gambling and making blasphemous oaths? Did she worship graven images, covet what she should not have coveted? After the film ended, the program's supervisor addressed the assembled masses to explain the significance of the "purgatory" bit. She didn't necessarily address the logistics of it—she seemed confident that all us Catholic kids had a guaranteed ticket to the top floor—but she did explain how we could help those souls who were not so fortunate. She suggested that whenever we suffered, whenever we stubbed a toe or flunked a test or writhed at the pleasure of an ineffable, uncaring god, we could process that suffering into a karmic coupon and offer it to someone trapped in purgatory, relieving a little bit of their debt in the process. We could be Jesus in miniature, carrying a fun-size cross to shave five minutes off of some bastard's poor afterlife sentence.

Thus I was initiated into the market of Christian redemption. Suffering, I learned, was currency. It was productive; it could be earned and traded in for fabulous prizes. Whenever you were miserable, whatever the cause, you were compounding interest on your angelic nest egg.

My spiritual scouring prevented me from developing a healthy, sophisticated system of ethics. Alcohol? Never! Jesus Christ never drank alcohol, and surely not before he was of legal age. Swearing? Certainly not! Jesus Christ would never have used language that might have upset or challenged his superiors; Jesus was a good Catholic boy. Sex? *Under no circumstances whatsoever.* Jesus Christ would never, say, fake his own death in order to cultivate a distorted messianic persona, then run off with some strumpet to propagate a divine bloodline that would be protected through millennia by the Knights

Templar. If my mind wandered during my religious education classes, I would sooner or later realize that I had set idols before God and then break into tears. My mother would try to comfort me, claim she didn't think I would actually bow before the fossilized visage of the blasphemous Carnotaurus and offer it my soul. But I was never sure. Also, due to a botched sexual education class I somehow became convinced that any contact between my hands and genitals constituted masturbation, and so many a ruinous itch went unscratched for fear of the mighty crotch-watching wrath of the vengeful Lord. It was not enough to be good, I decided. I had to become immaculate.

What confounded me in all of this was the fact that I was told over and over again that God loved me, and that God would forgive me for what I did wrong. I was supposed to love God more than anyone else, even more than I loved my family. How could I love someone so cruel and distant? God didn't love me. God hated me. He hated me the same way he hated everyone, and with good reason, because we were all fucking disgusting. And so, as a child, I hated God back. I hated him, but I respected him and I was afraid of him, and I prayed that this was enough.

The disorder, in its way, set about ensuring that I would be among the saved. It permitted only clean, sensible, religious thinking. It must be understood, in

Catholic tradition, that the thought is considered as bad as the deed. To contemplate a sin, according to Catholicism, is as spiritually perilous as committing it. "Thou shall not covet thy neighbor's property," said Moses, reading from the rock. "Thou shall not covet thy neighbor's wife." And I can guarantee, at that exact moment every person in the audience was plagued with horrible, irrepressible images of themselves shtupping the shiksa next door, probably while riding their neighbor's sweet new camel and eating delicious leavened bread. All thoughts are normal, I have learned since, and in attempting to suppress a thought it is inadvertently reinforced. But despite 250,000 years of evidence to the contrary, the Catholic Church stubbornly perpetuates an alternate psychological model, one that emphasizes traditional values and clean thinking, one literally chiseled into stone.

When I was about ten I somehow got it into my head that if I, for whatever reason, thought out the sentence "I promise my soul to the devil" in its entirety, I would be immediately and irreversibly damned. This hypothesis was not something I could prove or disprove. Christ never deigned to descend from heaven to assure me that I was in error. So, without definitive evidence either way, the disorder concluded that my theory had to be correct. If I allowed myself to think those seven words in sequence, my eternal soul was forfeit, just like that, and I would go to hell. Of course, though prohibited from dwelling on damnation, my mind fixed on it obsessively. I spent the better part of a Saturday afternoon completing my chores and doing homework, attempting to ignore these heretical figments; as difficult as it can be to steer your mind away from a taboo subject, it is almost but not quite impossible to catch it and mute it before it can finish a particular sentence. I kept a maddening silent vigil, each time interrupting my brain before it could finish the curse, but never able to end its perverse repetition. I promise my soul to the. I promise my. I promise my soul to. Over long hours I tried and failed to will myself saved.

In my desperation I occasionally attempted to circumvent the religious hierarchy and to present my queries directly to the Man himself. As honest and as frank as I was in these conversations I rarely found them satisfying. I remember one night in particular, during a family vacation on Cape Cod, when in a special moment of religious despair I walked out to the moonlit beach in hopes of obtaining counsel. I defy anyone not to experience something resembling awe when standing on a beach at night. Half of the world is a dark sky, often starless; of the other half, only part is safe and comfortable and lit by electricity, because starting at your feet and expanding to the horizon is black unbroken water. This is a full 75 percent of the sphere that is completely beyond human comprehension. Without malice, without will or conscience, yet capable of swift obliteration at any moment. Cold death above you and death before you. I spoke to God that night, as honestly and as thoroughly as I could. I explained to him my doubts, my fear, I professed what I believed to be the unshakable core of my faith. And then, as I turned to leave, a single shooting star crossed the sky.

I was certain, that night, that my supplication had been received and that my religious agonies were at an end. It was such a clear and unmistakable sign of God's presence, his acknowledgment of my struggle and his boundless forgiveness. I would years later, in college, receive what I took to be another sign from God, although under different circumstances and with different consequences—conditions that suggested not mercy but absolute judgment. In any case, despite my immediate sense of release, the obsession ultimately did not relent. I was relieved, perhaps, for a little while. When religious fixations threatened I would remind myself that I Had Seen a Sign from God and therefore Everything Would Be Okay. This was my attempt to construct a sensible narrative conclusion for my agonies. I rarely found it convincing.

The strangest thing, however, was that even as I struggled to appease God, I could never practice Catholicism with complete conviction. I could never shake those early doubts. My mother, a sporadic practicing Catholic but not an especially spiritual person, once compared the church to a salad bar. You had to pay attention only to the things that you believed in, and you could ignore the rest. I respected how my mother could be moderate and even-headed about such complex issues, but I couldn't agree with her on this. Religion isn't salad. I believed, or I was taught to believe, in a world without moral complexities.

An institution is right or it is wrong. One that cannot accept dinosaur bones is one that cannot be trusted on more important matters. Later I would find other grounds on which to question Catholicism and its influence over me, but this was what first caused me to doubt; this was what prevented me from ever really becoming a believer. An organization that cannot accept the physical realities of our universe is not one that I am comfortable accepting spiritual counsel from. Everything must be true, because otherwise anything could be a lie. There is no room for error when one claims to possess the word of God.

So I lived, uneasily, in a place of constant doubt. Even after I officially denounced my faith I felt a little twinge of guilt when I woke late on Sunday mornings, stumbling to breakfast in my pajamas. For a long time, I continued to say a silent Our Father every night before I went to sleep, lying in bed with my eyes shut and my hands pressed together. I wonder, sometimes, to whom exactly I was praying. Yahweh? Allah? Buddha or Vishnu? The great god Cthulhu who lies in R'lyeh dreaming? The mighty Tyrannosaurus Rex? Delirium of the Endless, celestial patron of the eternally confused? Or to nothing? Out into the darkness and the emptiness. I could not have explained why I continued to pray. But I did, for some time, and every night my last moments before sleep were filled with anxiety. Worried that my words were without purpose, that no one could hear them—terrified that somewhere, something or someone did.

3

Germ-free Adolescence

"All these people," said Japhy, "they all got white-tiled toilets and take big dirty craps like bears in the mountains, but it's all washed away to convenient supervised sewers and nobody thinks of crap any more or realizes their origin is shit and civet and scum of the sea. They spend all day washing their hands with creamy soaps they secretly wanta eat in the bathroom."

—Jack Kerouac, *The Dharma Bums*

As I grew older the apocalypse scenarios that had occupied me as a child lost their potency. (The exception here is the zombocalypse, which maintains a certain fascination. In idle moments I find myself pondering escape from ravenous undead hordes.) I never convinced myself they were impossible, but as time passed they became less immediately threatening. I learned to accept the possibility of the end of the world, and to live with it instead of denying it. Besides, I had survived puberty,

I was entering high school, and I would soon awaken to possibilities far more horrible than the extinction of all life on the planet.

Tell me: Does anyone really enjoy high school? Oh, I suppose if you looked you could find some university fratwit with treasured memories of getting blasted on shoplifted vermouth and banging fourteen-year-olds without fear of legal repercussion. But the rest of us nurture memories of swirlies, stand-ups, acne and bile. People expect pain in high school. Adolescence has escalated, and this makes things difficult for writers of memoirs. I could have carved pentagrams into my wrists with dirty syringes, and my suffering would evoke no more sympathy than a Very Special Episode. Somehow I am somehow supposed to differentiate between the ordinary, healthy misery experienced by a normal adolescent, as American as God and underage drinking, and the regressive, self-destructive misery inflicted by mental illness.

The only medically confirmed trauma I endured as a teen I endured twice, first at the end of middle school, and then again during high school. It started when I noticed that it was becoming difficult to eat any food of significant height, because my mouth was not opening as widely as it once had. For weeks I vainly mashed bagel sandwiches up against my just-parted teeth in a sorry attempt to absorb nutrition. The doctors took some X-rays and learned that my coronoid processes had hyperextended; the bones that hinged my jaw to my skull had overgrown and were fusing together into new unworkable joints. Without radical surgery the bones would have locked together permanently. I recognize now with a shiver that had I lived a century ago and somehow survived adolescence without killing myself, I would probably have starved to death with my mouth soldered shut.

I went through surgery twice. Each time my cheeks were cut open and the extraneous chunks of bone were extracted. After the first round the bones continued to grow, apparently stimulated by my rapid muscle growth, but after the second my surgeon hit on the brilliant, unconventional technique of paralyzing my facial muscles with Botox. Although I doubt I will be the last of my high school class to have his face injected with this deadly toxin, I took some sick pride in my certainty that I was the first. It was probably the only time I was the first to do anything in high school.

To help prevent my jaws from fusing together again, I was instructed to perform unique physical therapy. My doctor gave me a large box of medical tongue depressors. I was supposed to place as many of these as I could between my front teeth and bite down. Then I would take another and carefully force it into the middle of the stack, levering my mouth farther open by a fraction of an inch. I was told to repeat this until I had pried my mouth open to the greatest angle possible, and then to remain like this so that my jaw would have time to realign properly. The process was, as you can imagine, both embarrassing and very painful. Also, the crusty saliva on the used tongue depressors and the pools of mucus that condensed in the back of my throat during the therapy significantly increased my chances of catching cold. There! I've provided the skeptical reader with an incidence of undisputable, if ridiculous, medical tragedy.

If you ignored the problems with my head and my mind, I probably looked very much like any other emotional teenage pantywaist. I had shaggy hair, I wore flannel, and my face was a fleshy minefield. I did not ask girls out but instead stared at them for hours across history class, trying to establish subconscious rapport. I wrote terrible poetry and I drew bloody eyeballs emerging from wrists, and frequently I would lock myself in the third-floor bathroom and huddle shirtless on the floor, sobbing silently. You are repulsed? You recognize the cliché, the banal angst, and you are inclined to laugh. Believe me, I understand. What a pathetic, miserable fucker I was! But remember, my adolescent unhappiness was triggered not by the neurochemical imbalance of puberty, but by an entirely different set of neurochemical imbalances attributable to mental illness. So we all need to suppress our loathing for this cringing teenage gollum and establish some quantum of sympathy, or at least pretend to.

OCD is not inclined to unusual display. It works quietly and diligently to perpetuate the misery of its host. Not once as a teenager did I hallucinate, inflict bloody self-injury, commit any act that might have suggested that something was wrong. I never managed a single unnecessary public hand wash. To my many observers, up to and including professional therapists, my symptoms were indistinguishable from classic adolescent unhappiness. Without any standard of sanity to measure myself against, I had no idea how completely my brain was broken. The voice of the disorder, insidious and inescapable, was indistinguishable from my own.

I attended the tragically, gloriously named Beaver Country Day School in Chestnut Hill, Massachusetts. I regret that I need to identify the institution by name, because I don't necessarily hold a grudge against it and I'm sure it's a fine place to go to school if you aren't crippled by mental illness. But that name! That wonderful, horrible name! It filled my education with all kinds of idiotic double entendres. Some of these were accidental, like the running shirt that read BEAVER CROSS COUNTRY. Others were clearly intentional, like when the student council sold superfan athletic fundraiser shirts that read COME PLAY IN OUR DAM. The administration, to be fair,

seemed to become increasingly aware of the sexy implications of the school's name over time. Apparently, every
year, an unsuccessful appeal is put before the alumni board
petitioning to rename the institution BCDS. I imagine
it will never succeed because no one wants to explain to
a bunch of old blue-haired Jewish ladies the precise sexual
implications of the word *beaver.*

I arrived at the Beav' in seventh grade, fresh from my
hippie antieducation at my private elementary school. I
immediately experienced predictable social turmoil,
most of it too stupid to relate here, involving delicate
misinterpretations of the word *like.* Although my intrusive thoughts occurred only intermittently, the disorder influenced my behavior profoundly. Occasionally it
would manifest in obvious ways, cleaning and counting, although never blatantly enough to be recognized
as mental illness. I checked and rechecked. Once I stopped
in the middle of the school's foyer, suddenly uncertain
as to what direction I should keep walking in. I spun in
place for perhaps half a minute before cruel and unexpected laughter drew me back to reality. But usually
the disorder was less obvious than this, less visibly absurd, far subtler in its machinations. As a young adult I
was permitted no uncertainty: academic, ethical, social,
or otherwise. I expected perfect grades on every assignment. Although I was rarely tempted, I flatly prohibited
myself from any indulgence in sex, drugs, or drink, as I

believed them to demonstrate deficiency of character. In the single most unbelievable element of my narrative so far I will confess to you now: I did not masturbate, even once, until my second semester of college. Not once. When my dad tried to explain the procedure to me, I was repulsed. "You do *that*? Just for *sexual pleasure*?" I asked. "That's *disgusting*." This was the extent of my neurosis, so powerful and inescapable that it could prevent an otherwise healthy American adolescent from playing with himself. I would be pure, I would be perfect, or I would kill myself trying. Failure was intolerable.

I had many crises of heart and conscience, as my friends and acquaintances fell to predictable adolescent temptations: drug and drink were consumed, oral sex performed in bathrooms by and upon parties below the legal age of consent. This would have left any normal teenager unperturbed. Yet I was petrified. Each dumbass scandal propelled me into a crisis of conscience. Could I still remain friends with Johnny Asshat, even though he had knowingly brought a bottle of banker's vodka to school in his knapsack? Could I ever feel the same way about Jenny Promiscuity, who had bestowed intimate manual favors upon a classmate in the back of the bus one bright fall afternoon? I demanded of myself nothing less than complete asceticism, and whenever one of my classmates violated my unspoken, impossible standards, I felt I had been personally betrayed. A strange queasiness overtook me, as I recognized that my peers were entering new realms of experience; places that terrified me, places I myself could never enter.

Strangely, I had some not insignificant difficulty living up to the draconian standards of the tiny, petulant dictator who lived inside my brain. So in the absence of self-respect I learned, in my own subtle way, to suck up to adults like a deer tick. Authority figures were terrific and wonderful, because they would tell you exactly when you did something right. The people at the OCD Institute at McLean Hospital would later tell me that this behavior is called "people pleasing," and that it is common among obsessive-compulsives who struggle with perfectionism and low self-esteem. Since I did not like myself I needed to be certain that others liked me. I lived breathlessly awaiting the next gold star, the next homework pass, the dinosaur sticker from the dentist that legitimized my skilled use of mouthwash. I loved Big Brother, utterly and without irony.

My strategy worked surprisingly well with adults (He's so polite! Such a hard worker!), but was ineffective among the edgy teenagers-with-attitude who were my peers. Just like my teachers, my classmates had the terrifying power to accept or to reject me, and so my disorder coded them with unearned authority. Although I secretly despised many of them, the possibility that any one of them might have returned that dislike was intolerable. I was forced to forgive them, again and again, because a lasting, visible grudge would have been a dangerous demonstration of personality. I can imagine myself gazing fondly at the snarling, booze-addled mug of a fellow tenth grader. "Look at that face!" I'd say, and tweak a zit-lined cheek as he took a swig of vodka and Gatorade. "I can't stay mad at you! I would very much like to stay mad at you, because you are a spoiled idiot parasite with no redeeming qualities, but I can't!" My need for affirmation only perpetuated my petrifaction. If I could not say something witty and brilliant and sycophantic in conversation I forced myself to remain silent, and as I tried to be likable I usually seemed mute and inconsolable. Overwhelmed by the need for validation, to say the right thing to people I disliked, I was silenced, and instead of being shunned I was mercifully ignored.

I had one close friend through middle school and the beginning of high school, although our relationship quickly soured. We called him Timmy, even though that wasn't his real name, which should give you some idea of his appearance. He looked like a Timmy. He was small and childlike, with a tall stalk of hair, and as we progressed through adolescence he was afflicted with terrible acne. Timmy and I were both bright, and we shared a sense of humor, so we quickly developed a comfortable dynamic: He was the little bastard schemer; I was the tall straight man with the dry sense of humor. We ate lunch together, we talked about girls, and although I cannot remember us ever actually spending time together outside of school, he was the closest thing to a best friend I let myself have for some time.

Yet as high school began, and as adolescent tensions heightened, something in our relationship curdled. As I became more withdrawn, more repressed, Timmy realized that he could use me. Neither of us was especially popular, but Timmy recognized that it would increase his social cache to be seen bossing around someone taller and moderately more attractive than he was. Our friendship was sacrificed to the aid the social ambitions of this ridiculous little troll. I was no longer the straight man but the comedy sidekick. I could not attend class without hearing him chant my name in singsong fashion, soundtracked by my classmates' sniggering. Everything I said, no matter how banal, was cause for merriment. He acted as if my very existence were intrinsically amusing. Of course, Timmy still offered occasional gestures of genuine support and friendship, calculated to string me along, but he needn't have bothered. He was, like every one of my classmates, an authority. Even after I caught onto the con, I was powerless to resist it. Eventually my parents, recognizing that something was wrong, contacted the school and asked them to end Timmy's Machiavellian schemes. The consequences of this were predictable, and

I was blacklisted by Beaver's elite, even more so than before. Worst of all, I was deeply shamed that I had allowed myself to be so baldly snookered by someone called Timmy. There was something profoundly undignified about the whole mess.

My social anxiety also precluded dating. I did not date in high school. I did not engage in any activity that even superficially resembled dating in high school. I can remember with pristine clarity the moment when I first became interested in girls: I was watching television with my father and sister, and the program was interrupted by a commercial break. These were not sexy commercials. They were for minivans or for laundry detergent. But in a strange instant I found myself utterly mesmerized by the actresses' breasts. One moment they were breasts, and the next moment they were *breasts*. Without forewarning or explanation, these bags of flesh became fascinating, and not in a good way but in a queasy, tingling way that I did not understand and that made me really uncomfortable. Clearly these urges needed to be suppressed as aggressively as possible. I immediately resolved not to let my gaze rest upon these beguiling objects, for even a moment, and when this proved difficult I decided instead to fix my eyes steadfastly to the center of the screen. If boob happened to slip into my peripheral vision, well, fine, but otherwise I would not allow my viewing experience to be disrupted. Needless to say, these attempts did not succeed. In a way, though, they set the tone for my sexual experiences over the next decade of my life. The female body possessed a strange, irrational power, one to be isolated and controlled and delicately revered. If I were ever romantically interested in a girl, God forbid, I would woo her with respect and absolute discretion.

Romantic advice for neurotic young gentlemen: Girls like guys who are confident. Girls do not like guys who are polite, or gentle, or who supplicate themselves to the merest suggestion of an unintentional feminine whim, so utterly and aggressively prostrate as to open scabs on their knees and noses and grind streaks of blood into the carpet. Inasmuch as I was ever able to express affection, it was in insipid, pointless ways that I doubt even registered. I would stare for a moment longer than necessary; I would volunteer undesired aid in book lugging and door holding. Into these small crippled gestures were encoded volumes of terror and longing. But my feelings, confined and supercondensed as they were, were never requited. Boy-girl stuff consistently failed to occur.

I really had only one significant romantic possibility over the course of my teenage years, although her affections were unreciprocated. I met her in seventh grade, when I first transferred to Beaver. She was awkward and ungainly, and she admitted she suffered from bipolar disorder. We spent the rest of high school and a few weeks at a summer arts camp together, and through the years my feelings for her ranged from distaste to tolerance. But the entire time she had a hushed, furious crush on me. Her methods of seduction involved lots of staring and glancing, and occasionally proclaiming her love in a just-joking!-no-seriously-make-out-with-me manner. In retrospect, I think I got exactly the sort of lady admirer I deserved. She was like Fletcher for Fletcher. Her behavior around me differed from my own around girls that I liked only in that she was brave enough to attempt a final doomed demonstration of her passion.

My admirer left school to begin college a year early, and threw a good-bye party. As a gesture of goodwill I agreed to attend. I went with a mutual friend, and everyone enjoyed themselves, and my friend and I were leaving when I was accosted in the hallway by the hostess. "Fletcher," she asked, "can I ask you a question?" She then asked permission to kiss me. I said okay, recognizing that I would probably never see her again and expecting a brief, wistful peck. I was subjected to a passionate, highly concentrated one-person tactile makeout. I was left silent and stunned, unsure what exactly had occurred. Without warning I had received what was, with the technical exception of a few theatrical facsimiles, My First Kiss. On my personal list of Most Traumatic First Sexual Experiences this incident makes at least the top five. In any case she was gone after that, and I allowed my bemusement to curdle into an indignant and probably unjustified contempt.

Students at Beaver School were required to complete at least one semester of after-school athletics a year and, lacking basic hand-eye coordination, I signed up for cross-country running. It was a poor choice for several reasons. The largely individualistic nature of the sport discouraged me from bonding with my teammates, and my lanky, ugly adolescent body was not designed to be propelled over long distances at high speed. Most difficult were the long periods of exertion and isolation each afternoon during practice. I was asked to run alone, for several hours, slowly exhausting myself in the dull October weather. This was frequently a trigger for the disorder. Terrible thoughts occurred and I, alone in the autumnal suburbs, had no way of distracting myself from them. All I could do was keep running. Cross-country running is a lonely sport, but at times it can encourage a kind of Zen awareness, a pervasive peace of mind. Peace of mind was something I rarely enjoyed.

The rest of the year I acted in after-school theater. Fletcher, you ask, how could a miserable self-loathing bastard like your ever gather the confidence necessary to act like a total asshole in front of dozens of peers? Confession: Actually, I did not. The self-esteem I lacked in school and athletics did not magically manifest itself onstage. The absolute nadir of my career came in a tenth-grade production of *Cabaret*. I initially received a bit part as Bobby, the bisexual Nazi sympathizer, but the director had sinister designs on me that extended far beyond my unconvincing German accent. She had a second role in mind. She needed someone of a certain height, a certain build, someone who possessed a certain je ne sais quoi and no physical coordination whatsoever. Days before the show, I received my costume. It smelled of latex and was somewhat hairier than I'd expected. Imposing, yet frilly. I had been entrusted with a grave responsibility: I was being asked to play the dancing gorilla, and so I gave the role my utmost. I skipped, pirouetted, and frolicked across the stage with giddy abandon. In retrospect, I am mostly grateful that I got to wear a mask, an accessory that would have been useful during the rest of high school.

When I attained moments of relief it was, predictably, through videogames. Videogames were comfortably solitary, and more importantly, they had inviolable rules. They made sense when everything else refused to. Early in middle school, with no small amount of shame, I began to use Nintendo's Pokémon series. The game's rich, stupid mythology gave my imagination fertile soil to sow; their endless arithmetic of powerlevels and 2x weaknesses fed my OCD like cut cocaine. I would command my animal slave-soldiers to pummel the snot out of the same hapless digital caterpillar six hundred times, until one of them received some fractional increase in power, after which an equivalent rise would require 601 repetitions. This mechanic was comforting, and oddly familiar. I would continue for hours, until my hands or my chimerae seized from exhaustion.

I later developed a similar fixation on comic books. I was exposed to Neil Gaiman's *Sandman* series the summer after tenth grade. After my various disgraceful videogame addictions the series was like a fine absinthe: soothing, evocative, often fantastical. But *Sandman* was my gateway drug to the degrading spiral of Marvel and DC superhero comics, and eventually to the black tar heroin of Marvel's X-Men. The X-Men franchise, I have determined, has been developed with ruthless Darwinian precision to appeal to intelligent but lonely teenagers. The X-Men are mutant misfits shunned by regular society, just like you; the X-Men are also superpowered sexual demigods, demonstrably better than the normals who despise them because the normals can't shoot lasers from their eyes or extend razor-sharp Freudian claws from their knuckles. Therefore, by algebraic transitive property, you the reader are also a post-human sex god with eye lasers, and those stupid popula' kids are just too boneheaded to realize it! I like to think that I recognized the manipulative nature of this fantasy, although as when Cyclops submitted to psychic relationship counseling with the treacherous White Queen, my suspicions did not protect me from being seduced.

In the classroom I was rarely so consistently enthralled. To stave off boredom I learned to time bathroom breaks, with clockwork precision, halfway through each class period. If my teachers suspected drugs or persistent internal distress they never tried to intervene. I became something of a connoisseur of the bathroom, although not for reasons expected of obsessive-compulsives or hormonal teenage boys. Given my age and my usual level of stress, it should not surprise my readers that I often had grotesque acne, and in the bathroom I could tend to my lesions in relative privacy. My mother took it as a special responsibility to call me out every time she noticed that I had been picking at my face, hopefully to shame me into abandoning my little mutilations. Yet still I labored under the illusion that, if I farmed my blemishes aggressively enough, they could eventually be scraped away entirely. I hated the acne with perfectionist zeal. Over my four years of high school I accumulated a small armory of treatments; some of these were ingested, others were stored in the refrigerator until application, others were dyed so as to disguise blemishes and made me look as if I'd had topical makeup applied by a blind parakeet with a Q-tip. I saw a dermatologist, a terrifying woman with an icy demeanor who recommended exotic chemical treatments that did not, I was assured, have any demonstrable correlation with suicidal depression as confirmed by the FDA. Nothing worked. I slashed and seized at many a pustule, usually leaving the infection worse than it had been when I began. Most futilely, I once heard the popular myth that a person needed to consume eight glasses of water a day, and that doing so might help to clear my complexion; in typical obsessive-compulsive fashion I determined that this meant I would be better off consuming eight glasses of water eight times a day, which I am certain also played some part in my regular restroom visits.

But more importantly the bathroom was a refuge from my unending, desperate social performance. For ten, fifteen minutes I could stand, undisturbed, and pray that when I left the porcelain-tiled refuge everything would be better, that everything would stop hurting. I would galvanize myself, try to make myself invulnerable to the suffering outside. The bathroom usually contained a mirror, which was invaluable to my ritual declarations of self-loathing. I could leave class for a five-minute hate, spend a few moments gazing at my reflection and dreaming of punching it into shards of bloody glass. And then I could return, rejuvenated, restored.

When I was a child I thought it was called "sewerside." I thought that was where it happened, in the sewers, and that was where your body was discovered afterward. I had visions of sloping cartoon tunnels and rivers of glowing green filth, and a dead body lying motionless on a walkway to the side. The circumstances of the death were vague. I had no idea how a person would actually go about killing himself. I did not understand it as being related to pain or mental illness. I thought it was just something you chose to do, sometimes, for your own reasons. It was like throwing out an old coat. Sad, maybe irreversible, but without significant consequence. I remember in second grade my teacher told us she had sad news, about a big change in her life, and my first thought was that she had decided to kill herself. That tells you pretty much everything you need to know. Suicide was like changing a job, or like moving away. You'd tell your colleagues and pack your things, and then one day you wouldn't be there. You'd be gone.

I reached a point in high school where a day did not go by when I did not think of ending my life. I am not trying to quantify for you the extent of the pain I endured, or God forbid to brag about it; there is no meaningful form of human suffering that can be calculated in such a way, and if I tried to do so I would only demonstrate a lack of faith in the legitimacy of my experiences. Rather, I mention this to emphasize the enormous level of cognitive dysfunction that the human mind can be conditioned to endure. I might return home after school chipper and bright, beaming because I had told a joke everyone liked and I had thought of slitting my own throat only twice.

The suicidal impulses began innocuously enough, as an extension of my intrusive thoughts. When I was a child I would pass by a bridge or a tall building and repeatedly, helplessly imagine throwing myself off. As I aged I grew into deliberate suicidality. I thought about suicide constantly, often dispassionately. I entertained elaborate fantasies of public martyrdom, of being somehow present for my funeral, and of watching the endless procession of mourners who had scorned me in life realizing their terrible mistakes. These thoughts became an automatic psychological reaction to pain. When I hurt, I imagined dying. Without a counterexample, without a model of healthy psychological function, I barely even registered that anything was wrong. It just was something I thought about, something that I one day might choose to do.

My self-flagellation, any vague gestures toward self-harm, was never an end unto itself. I had been raised, like a good Irish-Catholic, to believe in the redemptive value of suffering, and in the absence of any significant external trauma I was determined to inflict the necessary damage myself. There were creative concerns to take into account, after all; I wanted to be a writer, and my middle-class Caucasian existence did not seem re-markable enough to justify this career. I had bought into that great, perverse myth that all artists need to experience extraordinary suffering in order to create interesting art. So I decided to make myself interesting. Not through education or self-improvement but by in-flicting as much pain on myself as I could stand. I was accumulating experience points, grinding levels, slowly bringing myself by intervals toward some unspecified end. Hoping desperately that one day I might grow strong and desperate enough to reach out and then without thinking leap the fence before I had time to stop my-self. Level-up. Evolve.

This was my mantra: I am human shit. I am human shit. It was my lullaby, my litany, my confession and penance. It has been written into my tongue, my lips, my teeth and jaw; I repeat it now, softly, and it is like slipping into a pair of old comfortable shoes. I mur-mured it in gentle tones through each day. I whispered it to myself each night as I fell sleep.

There were inevitably a few moments of minor ca-tastrophe, some of which my parents observed. Once in front of my mother I took a pair of scissors and held them, unopened, at my wrist. Another time I left the house without phone or keys with the intention of toss-ing myself off the nearest precipice, willfully ignoring the fact that there wasn't a building within five miles tall enough to ensure a thorough splatter. Sometimes I would drive myself to a highway overpass, park, and walk over to the arched chain-link fence that guarded the edges. I imagine it was there to prevent accidental tumbles, but I saw it as an absurd, almost insulting obstacle; if I was hurting so much that I wanted to kill myself, would I really let a short, mildly uncomfortable climb dissuade me? Would I arrive and suddenly decide that it would be easier to endure the rest of my meaningless, agonizing life than to climb over a six-foot fence?

Such moments of desperation were always triggered by utterly, infuriatingly mundane circumstances. I might receive a mediocre grade on a pop quiz, or overhear in the hallway a snide remark that must have been directed at me. The first major crisis came from the most trivial, most adolescent incident possible. I had had a difficult day, and then during play rehearsal that afternoon my mother came in to pick me up for an appointment. She merely opened the door and waved a bit for me to come outside. But I was not merely embarrassed. I was humiliated, I was devastated beyond all reason, and I entered a near-catatonic state of despair. Partway home, utterly noncommunicative, I attempted to open my door while the car was moving. I am not sure of my intentions. I did not unfasten my seat belt, nor was the vehicle moving with sufficient speed to result in any significant injury had I attempted to jump.

Hilarity! Frivolity! The poor suburban white boy traumatized by Mommy, tries to off himself! Sick little fucker! It was not my external circumstances, but my disproportionate and completely irrational psychological response to these circumstances, that caused my distress. I fully understood the inanity of my situation, and my understanding contributed to my pain and desperation. It didn't help. It made it worse. The fact that I was so completely psychologically fucked by this trivial shit was infuriating. I should have been stronger but I wasn't and I hated myself for it. From this perspective, perhaps a benign gesture such as opening a car door at an inappropriate time may be understood as an act of self-destruction.

I was taken to an emergency room that night. I have always had unreliable veins, and it took so many alcohol swabbings and needles to take a blood sample that when the doctor finally examined the sample he assumed that I was drunk. No, my mother informed him, he doesn't drink. I was sort of diagnosed with depression, which I accepted because whatever I was going through it sure as hell felt like depression, and told that I needed to start therapy.

My new therapist was friendly and swaggering; he encouraged me to take it easy on myself, to open up to others, to care less about what people thought of me. This was trite bullshit, but it didn't matter because I'd also started to see a psychiatrist. I am profoundly grateful for the role that medication has played in my recovery, and for the treatment administered to me by competent, sympathetic professionals. This man was not one of them. My parents and I met him in an old Victorian house that had been converted into an office building, and I can remember reading year-old *New Yorker* magazines as I waited to be treated. The psychiatrist had pale, leathery skin and a few wisps of light hair. His eyes were perpetually sleepy. His questions were often leading ones, as if he already knew the answers and he wasn't particularly interested in hearing me repeat them. I don't think I ever had a single meeting with him that lasted longer than fifteen minutes.

I had long resisted medication, for many of the same reasons that I shunned drugs and alcohol. It felt like cheating, like giving up. It seemed a sign of weakness. But I was no longer in any position to resist. My psychiatrist prescribed antidepressants and when these failed to resolve my problems he prescribed more of them. Lacking any kind of definite diagnosis he decided to toss Effexor at me and see what happened.

Effexor is a motherfucker of a drug. It has an absolutely ridiculous number of side effects. It is the psychopharmaceutical equivalent of nuking the site from space just to be safe. It was prescribed not because it was appropriate for my condition but because it was the drug most likely to obliterate my symptoms at minimal cost to my insurance provider. The side effects of the Effexor were immediate and impossible to ignore, although it is difficult now for me to articulate them, because they were defined as much by an absence of sensation as by its presence. I experienced a persistent discomfort not entirely unlike vertigo, a strangely hollow feeling—the nauseous recognition of empty places in one's mind. It was like the acute awareness of the absence of a headache, just slightly uncomfortable although not painful, like chewing a too-large piece of bubble gum that has lost its color and flavor. Ghost circles, psychic white noise.

I slept for absurd hours each night and ran traffic lights and slurred my words. My normally heroic metabolism, which had kept me lean and fit through most of high school despite my massive consumption of cheese-flavored snack crackers, slowed to an embarrassing crawl. But I began, unavoidably, to stabilize. I let myself make friends and fail quizzes. I started to write humorous essays and read them at assembly, which my peers and teachers seemed to enjoy and, encouraged by their praise, I began to consider the possibility I might actually be a worthwhile person. At one point, after consultation with my parents, I even chose to try alcohol at a friend's house, a decision that would have previously been unthinkable; my poor beleaguered liver subsequently short-circuited, and I passed out after a hard lemonade and a sip of gin. I awoke groggy soon after sunrise, pants soaked with piss, and drove home traumatized by the consequences of underage drinking. So my senior year of high school included a handful of pleasures and perils that vaguely resembled those experienced by a normal human teenager. In the end, I limped across the stage and took my diploma in a medication-induced haze.

It was finished. I had beaten high school. The game was over and I had won. I had faced my monsters and then lulled them into a narcotic coma, I was stable and sane and I would be forever. My family and I told ourselves that everything was all right now. The future was waiting. I was going to college.

4

Boys and Girls in Academia

Their infinity was more like the empty infinity of arithmetic, something unthinkable, yet necessary to thought. Or it was something like the stunning statements of astronomy about the distance of the fixed stars. He was ascending the house of reason, a thing more hideous than unreason itself.
—G. K. Chesterton, *The Man Who Was Thursday*

How's that working out for you? . . . Being clever?
—Tyler Durden, in *Fight Club*

I had started my college search in the spring of my junior year. The process was above all else spectacularly uninspiring. My parents, my younger sister, and I went on a grand tour of franchise hotels across the East Coast; we tested a dozen lukewarm swimming pools, gazed out a dozen windows at identical parking lots. We also visited some colleges, and while the schools were supposedly the focus of the trip they all sort of blurred together. We found ourselves silently wishing that our friendly, informative undergrad tour guides would, while walking backward, trip and break something, if only to relieve the monotony.

My senior year of high school continued, and even into second semester I had no idea where I wanted to go. My classmates, carefully guided by parents and hired advisers, had their futures determined with cold certainty by January. It was like watching an extraterrestrial mind-control invasion as, one by one, my classmates arrived at school with eyes glazed over. They became distant, detached, disinterested. They wore bright hooded sweatshirts with their future university's name, the fabric thick and plasticky, like an alien symbiote. The semester progressed, and even as I returned to several of the schools I'd liked I couldn't find a favorite; although Wesleyan was dropped from serious consideration when a classmate told me, deadpan, that she was dating a guy there and that the students were "all really into needle drugs."

I came to Swarthmore College almost arbitrarily. It was the last school I visited, during the Ride the Tide event, a student-admissions weekend named in honor of the increasingly nonexistent Garnet Tide sports team. Swarthmore was founded in 1864 by Quaker educators, and the school is home to the renowned Scott Arboretum; while the sheer variety of plant life ensured that some allergy would be triggered in each student, I was enchanted by the lush campus. Yet the most striking feature of the college's landscape was neither foliage nor architecture, but furnishing. On the front lawn of the school were clustered white wooden Adirondack chairs, identical except for one. This was the big chair. Perfectly scaled up from its smaller cousins, just too large to be functional, frequently covered by small visiting children or freshmen. It had a kind of surreal majesty.

I was soon scooped up by my assigned student host, who helped me lug my stuff up to his room and then took me on a guided tour of the campus. This focused less on important campus landmarks and more on oral autobiography, a lovingly detailed history of everywhere on campus that he had gotten high. He led me from dorm to shrub to women's resource center. This took most of the day, and by the end I had concluded that most of the arboretum plants had narcotic properties, if only because of the ambient toxicity of atmosphere. Still: no needle drugs.

This tour was by default the most interesting part of my visit. I attended a class, I made nervous conversation with other visiting students over dinner, and then I went to bed. Yet I thought as I lay awake, prone in a sleeping bag on an unwashed floor among strewn underwear and a three-foot bong: I wanted to be a writer, and writing is a difficult and demanding profession. It would behoove me, then, to choose an institution with both a rigorous curriculum and a reputation for academic badassery. I needed every advantage I could get. True, the students here seemed either dull or faintly desperate, but surely no social experience could be worse than the one I was leaving behind.

My mother appeared at the door the next day around noon. She was greeted by a grunt and a half-conscious wiggle from my host, who was surly and semiconscious that morning for reasons upon which I will not speculate. Together my mother and I gathered my things and left. Driving away, the two of us discussed the school, and she asked me if when I'd arrived on the campus it had felt like I was coming home. It hadn't. The question was a little presumptuous. But Swarthmore felt as close to home as any of these places had, and I decided that if I was serious about going there I would have to psyche myself up. So, yes, I told her. Sure. This place was home.

With self-inflicted jubilance my mother and I spun around and rushed back to the school store, looking for official regalia I could stamp myself with. I chose a pair of T-shirts. The first of these read THE PEOPLE'S REPUBLIC OF SWARTHMORE, and was printed with a hammer and sickle: a dig at the inexplicable liberal politics of liberal arts colleges, very humorous, all well and good. But the other shirt, I believe, deserves special attention. The other shirt featured the official Swarthmore College logo and then read in a large clear font: GUILT WITHOUT SEX.

This was the school I chose. This was the place I decided was home. Guilt Without Sex. As an embittered semi-Catholic celibate the phenomenon described was not unknown to me. I appreciated the bitterness, the implicit self-deprecation, although it was never explained what in the absence of sex I was supposed to feel guilty about. When I returned to high school, if a classmate or a bemused teacher asked what the slogan meant I could only shrug. I didn't get the joke, either. There was nothing to get. While I could not explain it to the uninitiated, it still resonated. There was something, I knew, that I needed to feel guilty about. I didn't understand it, but maybe that was what I was going to Swarthmore for. Maybe there I could find out.

I remember my first days at Swarthmore. My mother's minivan, Valkyrie-like, deposited me at the threshold of my new home. College was supposed to be my Valhalla, my New Genesis; my arrival should have been a divine homecoming, an ascent to the halls of Olympus after years of purgative pubescent hell. I would take classes that engaged and challenged me. I would socialize not with preppy assholes but with the intellectual asshole elite. I would complete my first five novels and meet my future wife. I had left my problems behind like so many discarded SAT prep books. Here I would begin a golden, glorious future.

But something was off. My classmates were intelligent and friendly and within three weeks I hated all of them. And sadly the rumors I'd heard of the homeliness of Swarthmore's student body did not seem entirely scurrilous, which I was concerned could delay my discovery of my eternal soul mate. Still, I remained confident. I had overcome all of my problems through persistence and sheer force of will, and enough antidepressants to kill a rhinoceros. This school was the perfect place for me, and no amount of contradictory evidence would convince me otherwise.

The freshman orientation process was a queasy blur, all drama games and library tours, the faculty offices taking every opportunity to shower us with mugs and trinkets. The singularity of Swat was emphasized to us repeatedly through a series of orientation-slash-indoctrination sessions; we were told that would enjoy an incomparable academic experience at Swarthmore, at once exhausting and coddling, accommodating the awkward and the socially incompetent alike. We were told, again and again, that we would be challenged at Swarthmore. We would be asked to call our professors by their first names, which would make us feel very uncomfortable. We would laugh, cry, learn lessons that would last a lifetime, cry, and suffer. Oh sweet Jesus Christ in heaven, we would suffer!

The sophomores and juniors, deadened by their long semesters of bleak living, luxuriated in telling us of the academic trials that awaited us. Eyeing our supple freshman bodies, they told us that Swarthmore made Spartan military training look like a year in Alpha Bromega at SUNY Albany. The school was like getting strapped to a giant Adirondack chair with your eyelids pried open and then watching endless PowerPoint slide shows while old Ludwig Van played in the background. Like being tied to a rock and then whipped with spiked chains, each link inscribed with the full text of Hobbes's *Leviathan*: Our education would be solitary, poor, nasty, brutish, and short. Swarthmore was not a college, we were told, and despite what the admissions department would cheekily suggest, Swarthmore was not a way of life. It was like a memetic virus or a cult. Swarthmore was an atrocity. It was unending agony, decaying the body, draining the will to live. So it was said.

These are all jokes that I am weary of repeating. I heard them countless times over my four years at the school, from friends and classmates and occasionally even from the professors and administrators. Although they were not incisive observations, no one seemed to tire of them, and they could always be counted on for a bitter yet oddly affectionate laugh. Indeed, I spent years embellishing these jokes to the point of self-parody; much of this chapter is revised from a newspaper column I published my sophomore year, enhanced with a subtextual layer of bitterness and regret. Swarthmore jokes were easy because Swarthmore jokes were safe, because enmity toward Swarthmore was the foundation of the Swarthmore cult. The atom of Swarthmore, the fundamental particle from which all of our social interactions were constructed, was this: two students approaching each other and each complaining about the school and then both falling into mutual embarrassed silence with nothing else to say.

This attitude was so pervasive that it developed its own idiom. It was a game. We called it "misery poker," and it was perhaps the only universal pastime at the school. Every class, every activity, was granted an unspoken but universally agreed-upon denomination, a point value based on the sum of the personal unhappiness it inflicted. Other benefits, any personal or intellectual enrichment derived, were secondary. All that mattered was how much it hurt. So at lunch and in classes and dorms, we held up hands in front of our faces and exchanged shifty glances. We exaggerated and extolled our burdens to imply total unhappiness. We all went along with this self-destructive dick waving, desperate to demonstrate that our selflessness and individual commitment to the life of the mind were quantifiably greater than that of our fellow students.

Of course, there was more to life at Swat than work. Social interaction was also popular in certain restricted circles. Music was an integral part of my experience at Swarthmore: The school hosted indie rock and a cappella concerts, student a cappella groups and indie rock bands, and a radio station with a robust selection of a cappella and indie rock. Yet strangely, in an environment populated by the bright and the lonely, the power of music was evoked almost exclusively as an instrument of hate. Most musicians performed in Olde Club, a drafty shack of a building, its foundations so permeated with spilled mixers and clove cigarette smoke as to threaten collapse. Almost every moderately known artist I saw perform at Olde Club did so begrudgingly, wooed by the possibility of merchandise sales or free sex, and the concerts had an unpleasant sameness to them. The androgynous singer would sneer at his pale congregation, and the audience would sweat in meticulously disheveled layers of vintage fabric, sneering right back. After the show everyone would loiter, holding cans of cheap beer, dissecting the performance and dismissing one other. Everyone hated everyone else, a vicious circle spinning like a vinyl record, a feedback loop of contempt. I expect this kind of anger in more aggressive, sociopathic genres of rock music. But to find this same confrontational attitude in privileged nerds who wrote and performed music exclusively for other privileged nerds was a little baffling.

Extracurricular activities were effectively mandatory at Swarthmore. After all, even if you saturated your schedule with classes and homework, there were still several hours a day available for furious intellectual masturbation. Upon arrival at Swarthmore, we were assaulted by any number of clubs and activities. Student council at once developed from high school student government—and prepared us for real-world politics—by manifesting itself as a spectacularly uninformed popularity contest. There were a number of art galleries on campus, and although you never had time to actually visit these, the little glossy postcards handed out to advertise new exhibits looked sort of cool if you put them on your corkboard. Sports fans thrilled to campus athletics, with attendance for individual events sometimes flirting with the double digits.

And despite boasts of our moral intelligence, like all college students the Swarthmore discontented were easily silenced by booze and circuses. In the absence of popular athletics, the competitive spirit at Swarthmore manifested in much stranger, more rigidly codified forms. Among these was the annual Pterodactyl Hunt, where dozens of Swatties gathered to fulfill a lifelong ambition and, for one brief, magical evening, transform their lives into something resembling The Legend of Zelda: Ocarina of

Time. The game was endearingly complex and unrelentingly geeky. Its labyrinthine rules involved rival factions of orcs and trolls, upgradable weapons, upgradable weapon upgrades, and a unique zoology of slayable monsters encompassing everything from hydras to samurai to ninja turtles. The infamous pterodactyl functioned as a sort of final boss, equipped with Super Soakers and an army of bodyguards, and whoever successfully felled it was granted a boon that could be exchanged at the local pizzeria for a large pie. With the exception of my junior year, when regrettable circumstances prevented me from attending, I participated in the Pterodactyl Hunt every year, and most of the time it was a lot of fun. Only occasionally did Swarthmore overenthusiasm cloud the proceedings. The costumes for the gratuitous "vampire," "sexy cat girl," and "other sexy cat girl" monsters bordered on the fetishistic, and without being overly judgmental I will say that these creatures were generally portrayed by students from whose erotic fantasy life I would have happily remained excluded. Inevitably, some participants would take the proceedings far too seriously, sprinting across the field to stab an unaware rival in the back and then, stone-faced, demand their poker-chip bounty. But for the most part the hunt was good-natured, a harmless evening of silly fun.

Infinitely more troubling was Crunkfest, an annual tradition established my freshman year. Named after an obsolete genre of hip-hop or something, Crunkfest soon became an annual rite of spring at Swarthmore. It was a twenty-four-hour bacchanalia, with public nudity and sexy activity, epic consumption of narcotics and occasional moments of inspired absurdity. One year saw an improvised passion play performed by a squad of religion majors, their tipsy Christ hobbling with a cross on his back and a can of beer taped to his stomach; this was later pierced by a spear-wielding centurion, and the brew that issued forth from his side was collected in a grail. Almost every year someone would try to legally change his middle name to Crunk. Some years required temporary tattooing with ballpoint pens in a way that superficially resembled self-mutilation, which made me queasy for personal reasons, but understand that I had no complaint against the spirit of Crunkfest. Nudity and gratuitous substance abuse in college are part of an ancient and venerable Belushian tradition. No, my problem with Crunkfest was that the entire absurd spectacle was a fucking *competition*. All were judged and subsequently ranked for their enthusiasm and creativity in drinking, smoking, circle-jerking, shitting-in-the-taco-mart et cetera. Swarthmore culture apparently could not sustain an anarchic Dionysian orgy unless an arbitrary academic structure was imposed over it. God forbid someone should get high and run around naked if they couldn't get points for doing so. How could you be certain that what you were doing was fun if you weren't being assigned numbers for it?

Swarthmore was not a place, I learned, where you did things halfway. An assigned text should be completed weeks in advance or given only a cursory glance minutes before class. A body should subsist either on minimal vegan fare or on fried egg sandwiches and midnight pizza. Tipsy was never preferable to wasted or to self-righteous sobriety. No matter how much you did it was never enough: You must always study more, self-deprecate and -flagellate more, party and drink and fornicate more, work more so that you can complain more. Do enough and whine enough and you can beat your friends, you can win college, and you will earn from your peers sympathy and accolades and silent, seething contempt. Swarthmore was a place of uncompromising, delirious extremes. It took intelligent young people at the cusp of adulthood, unusually sensitive and self-motivated, and demanded from them performance beyond any reasonable standard. It isolated our worst qualities (self-abuse, introversion, passivity, inappropriate intellectualization) and shamelessly encouraged them. It taught us to nurture them, to recognize and chuckle affectionately at them. Adulthood, to say nothing of an education, cannot be attained under such circumstances. We learned to be pointlessly cruel to ourselves and to be proud of it.

Some of you will suggest that I am projecting my

own neurosis onto the institution. You may be correct; there are obvious reasons to doubt my capacity for clear and objective thinking. But I don't believe I am.

Chief among my own extracurriculars freshman year were regular appointments with a counselor. She was pleasant, gentle, and sympathetic, and like all of my previous therapists she was somehow oblivious to the disorder. She encouraged me to call her by her first name, but still in awe of adult superiority I referred to her as "Doctor," actual credentials irrelevant. Over months of painfully superficial analysis we explored the shallowest depths of my psyche. My problems were apparently as follows. One: I had issues with my parents. Two: I had issues with relationships, especially romantic or sexual ones. Three: I was too hard on myself. She was content to review these points once a week, and by way of guiding counsel she reminded me at intervals to (one) not care so much, (two) relax, and (three) stop being too hard on myself. This was as correct as it was simplistic, but in any case it was insufficient to overwrite the cognitive mechanisms I had excruciatingly constructed over nineteen years of mental illness; the therapeutic equivalent of giving a Snoopy bandage to a victim of flesh-eating parasites.

This is not to say that I did not enjoy parts of my freshman year. I got decent grades, although they rejected my application for the spring fiction workshop. I half-assed several minor community service projects and hosted a weekend radio show with an audience: my mom. I even joined a sketch comedy troupe, with whom I developed an unbreakable, ever-creepier bond. The group was called Boy Meets Tractor, after a romantic subgenre of Soviet propaganda. The previous year had seen the graduation of the founding members of the troupe, and I was admitted along with a score of other confused, blinking freshmen. We met several times a week to write, and on Saturdays to shoot interminable video sketches. Although, looking back, I find the lack of coherent editing or jokes in these early videos to be a little embarrassing, our material improved over time. And most important, Boy Meets Tractor gave me the opportunity to work, regularly, with people whom I did not immediately hate, on something that we all cared about. I found myself in a situation where, try as I might, I could not avoid making friends, and I eventually developed an easy intimacy with my fellow amateur comedians. We became close, and as my mental state degenerated they became something of a lifeline for me.

Of course there were a handful of other extracurricular activities, for various reasons unavailable in high school, that I started to explore. It was at Swarthmore, in this den of fascists and maniacs, that I made my first, few pitiable attempts to breed.

5

Losing It

I have tried to give you a sense of what it was like for me at Swarthmore, and yet I have left out a significant part of student life. It was college, after all. There was sex. This shouldn't be entirely unexpected. It is a truth universally acknowledged, and supported by a canon of soft-core pornography, that college students are interested in sex. But surprisingly, my observations have indicated that this interest is not exclusive to pert and bi-curious state-school hardbodies. Geeks are also really intrigued by sex, their enthusiasm intensified by the scarcity of opportunities they have to enjoy it. So the intersection of these two demographics at Swarthmore, this legion of young geeks in love, produced a perfect storm of thwarted impulses. There was a staggering inverse between interest in sex and the ability to solicit and engage in it. Many of the conversations I observed while at Swarthmore were about sex. But, significantly, sex was the unacknowledged subject of every non-conversation: all the stuttering and blinking and looking away, the comments on the weather and the flowers in the spring, the touching and the desperate looks at parties. This was where I wanted to break my eighteen-and-a-half-year streak of celibacy. This was the place where I first kissed a girl, willingly, and outside of a high school play.

If nothing else, Swarthmore's low standards allowed me to climb several links up the sexual food chain. In this tense environment girls, inconceivably, began to respond to my person with neither pity nor contempt. My confidence was still crippled by the disorder; I held doors at keggers and cried after making love, but at Swarthmore I was a positive badass.

I attribute this entirely to the desolation of the Swarthmore singles scene. While many of us arrived there in reasonable health, the environment quickly took its toll. As fall semester passed a metamorphosis took place, like a butterfly's wings wilting back into its spine before it collapsed into a fat hairy caterpillar. Ruddy flesh faded to cadaverous hues. Acne and eczema spread across skin like red plastic soldiers. Any residual muscular tissue was broken down by the body for nutrients. In this demanding environment, where students were required to navigate a challenging schedule of courses, extracurricular activities, and hating themselves, it was easy to neglect basic hygienic practices; it was easy, in the dining hall, to snub the salad bar and instead succumb to the crusty temptations of delicious waffle fries.

But even if you did not realize that Swat students were not attractive you would quickly be told so. We loved to talk about how unattractive we were. I found that self-deprecation allowed me to, without actually committing to changing my lifestyle, at least demonstrate awareness of my poor health and punish myself for it, which was probably almost as good. Students became hideous so that we could mock ourselves for being hideous and date other hideous people. We were like the picture of Dorian Gray of American higher education, rotting in a dusty attic while the other schools enjoyed eternal decadent hotness. I quickly learned at Swarthmore that my standards for attractiveness were unrealistic, that each of us on the inside is a beautiful and compelling snowflake or something and that's what's really important; because no one was prepared to consider the troubling possibility that the ugliness was not necessarily entirely on the surface.

The school did have a small population of attractive and confident "mainstream" students, and woe to these rare, pitiful creatures. Like the Siberian tiger, they were hunted for their beauty by those who would cage and abuse them or gut them for the medicinal properties of their kidneys. At parties and in class you could spot them instantly, crowded with admirers appearing to represent several genders, orientations, and species; supplicants who clutched with horny fingers, teeth bared like those of a submissive chimp. The pretty kids at Swarthmore always seemed distant and nervous. Their genetic superiority condemned them to a life of voluntary chastity, scorning endless queues of meek and apologetic suitors. I remain hopeful that the school's administration may someday establish a sanctuary for these creatures, in order to build a stable breeding population and then introduce legacy students, born in captivity, back into the wild. But during my time these paradoxical collegiate unicorns—beautiful yet reluctant to be touched by virgins—were scarce.

Even the absence of physically attractive partners could not eliminate certain appetites. My freshman class was intelligent and highly motivated and we had diverse interests, and in high school most of us got less ass than a urinal. The possibility of erotic stimulation by any hand other than your own was terrifying and thrilling. Without actual experience, our erotic expectations were set by "Savage Love" advice columns, by naughty fan fiction, by high-school seminars involving latexy preparation of bananas. Bashful and young, most of us had two fundamentally irreconcilable objectives in mind. We wanted to find our soul mates, correlate, commingle, misconstrue, and reconcile sobbing in the rain, then eventually marry and raise children; and we wanted to make love in this club.

I saw college as a chance to start over with girls, unburdened by my accumulated years of adolescent discomfort. Besides, it was autumn when I arrived, and the leaves were falling and insects dying en masse, and from the life-denying perspective of Swarthmore freshmen there could have been no greater aphrodisiac. Yet I chose to take advantage of this opportunity by responding to women the same way I had since puberty. I was hardly alone in this. At classes and in libraries interest was always indicated in the same way: by an exchange of tentative glances and half smiles. Neither participant would be willing to risk the heartbreak of unrequited eye contact, and so the heads of the besotted whipped from side to side so rapidly as to induce motion sickness. This was usually as far as things went. No one was really very proactive when it came to dating. But short of actually starting a conversation, people tried everything else imaginable to lure mates into their personal bubbles. I saw people who studied online correspondence like gnostic gospels, trying to decode some hidden cryptogram of attraction; who started freshman hot lists in online forums and then would not contribute to them, apparently so tantalized by the possibility that hot freshmen could be listed that to actually list hot freshmen would be unimaginably decadent. On Valentine's Day people sent school-sponsored ninjas to attack their intended ("ninjagrams"), apparently having concluded that their feelings would be best expressed through anonymous mock assassination. You could look across the table at the dining hall and deep into the eyes of any supposedly platonic acquaintance, and you could be almost certain he or she was fantasizing about driving a minivan filled with your wailing brats, of sitting together on a porch in your twilight years, tenderly clutching withered hands and then suffering adorable simultaneous heart attacks.

Despite this crippled romanticism Swarthmore maintained a robust weekend singles scene, if by "robust" one means "creepy" and "monotonous." It was this seething hot plate of Quaker hormones that was responsible for most successful couplings. Parties were typically held in intimate, poorly lit venues such as the Delta Upsilon fraternity or Olde Club. Yet while events in either location were adequately sinful, neither came close to the infamy of the Paces café. The name won't mean anything to a non-Swarthmore student, but among students it evoked contempt and shame and forbidden, feverish desire. Consider the implications of the place's name. "Paces." Walking back and forth. Repetitive, recursive but frenzied activity, demonstrative of frustration, performed during a moment of unbearable anticipation for whatever it is you really want. The implications are not inappropriate. Four nights a week Paces was a late-night café, serving herbal tea and quesadillas that you would probably not have to pay for, because the staff was usually high and would forget about your order for like forty-five minutes and then waive the bill to apologize. But on Friday and Saturday nights the true spirit of the place manifested itself, the lights were dimmed and the shadows supplemented with smog and electric blurs, and dulled, pounding music could be heard across campus.

The adventurous could visit on any weekend night to observe pale, pockmarked students, struggling against years of social rejection and sexual repression, letting off some steam and enthusiastically grinding their pelvises into each other. Despite the loathing and disgust that many expressed for these parties, they were perpetuated by a tacit understanding of their social necessity. Many of us required not only alcohol but also the implicit approval of dozens of other sloppy couples, each publicly performing their own rendition of the vertical horizontal flamenco, in order to express what might have been conveyed by a scrap of paper: DO YOU LIKE ME CHECK YES OR NO. Assuming all the appropriate bumps and grinds were initiated, the couple could finally stagger off, usually losing momentum between secondary and tertiary bases.

There were moments when Paces etiquette was ignored, at events like the costumed Screw Your Roommate dance (thankfully almost always a meaningless double entendre, where you sent your roommate on a blind date wearing a silly costume) or the dreaded Genderfuck party (there is nothing you need to know that cannot be inferred from the name). The Halloween party was uniquely epic. Each year it was like a fever dream, the sort one might have after reading online fan fiction and then taking peyote. Videogame heroes, beloved figures from Generation Zero's collective childhood, risqué caricatures of politicians and exotic creatures from Japanese animation. All were replicated with fetishistic detail, removed from narrative context, and then set writhing and grinding in a hallucinatory clothed orgy. The event was held in the dining hall my senior year, so you could climb up to the balcony and look out over the whole spectacle. It was a manic fantasia, the crossover event you never dreamed. It could become tremendously upsetting around one in the morning or so, especially if you were drunk, which at this point you (i.e., I) probably were (i.e., was).

I can still remember my first college dance party with really inexplicable clarity. It was the first Friday after orientation, in Paces. That night I had a Coke and possibly rum. (Drinks at Swarthmore parties were like Schrödinger's cat: The alcohol existed in a state of quantum flux, simultaneously proof and nonproof.) That seemed to go okay, so I had a second and a third. This was not an overwhelming amount of alcohol, but the frankly stupid quantities of antidepressants in my bloodstream increased the drink's power exponentially. At some point I noticed a not unattractive girl from one of my classes making aggressive eyes at me. I approached her, I received my first authentic, consensual, nontheatrical kiss, and things proceeded from there.

OCD and sex: If a girl accepts an invitation to help count the tiles on your bedroom ceiling, she will probably be disappointed when she realizes you were speaking literally. I regret to say that the cumulative effect of the medication, the booze, the lack of experience, and the guilt and terror and desperation and self-loathing was entirely predictable. We learned the subtle but critical difference between "sexy side effects" and "sexual side effects." I awoke horrified the next day, alone in my own bed. Eager to make amends I immediately arranged a date for coffee, and when we met I apologized like sixty times over the course of twenty minutes. This behavior, needless to say, did not reignite the fires of our passion, and we spent the remainder of the semester exchanging painful non-glances from opposite sides of the classroom. This first romantic encounter set the stage for many of my freshman-year relationships: shame, social ineptitude, meaningfully ungratifying attempts at meaningless physical gratification. Pity our incompetent Lothario, in his noble but doomed attempts at idiot hedonism.

I quickly decided that instead of finding an actual girlfriend, it would be easier to be in unrequited love. I do not think I could have chosen a less appropriate target for my affections. The object of my devotion was a friend living on my hall, already dating an older student, either oblivious to or utterly uninterested in my mute infatuation. Alone, I indulged silent angst and insane hope, somehow dreaming that my nonexistent signals would convince her of our love. I was convinced that being meek and polite, being nice, would win the heart of my desired. This was the brilliance of the scheme: It excused me from actually asking her out. It was appealing because it required no risk; I was never exposed to the devastating possibility of "no." And it worked, it had to work, even if I understood it was unlikely, I wanted it so badly it had to work for me; and through

my strenuous noneffort I would find undying love. I
learned to brood and wilt silently, dismissing any possibility of building an actual relationship with someone else as a diversion, at the same time pursuing as
many superficial flings as possible to distract myself from
my doomed romance.

My experiences at that disastrous first party should
have scared me away from that sort of encounter. Alcohol had a predictably sedative effect on my enthusiasm
for romance, yet if I went to a party where I thought I
could meet someone I made certain that I was at least a
little sloshed. Part of my rationale, grounded in years of
doublethink and my still-simmering Catholic tendencies, was that I could never in good conscience allow
myself go home with someone who had been drinking
if I myself was sober. I found the idea of taking advantage of someone in this way to be completely abhorrent.
(Apparently I had no such reservations about allowing
myself to be taken advantage of.) But if both of us had
been drinking, or even better if I was the only one
who was drunk, everything was fine. The possibility of
an encounter during which both parties were sober, or
where nothing sexual happened until after several dates,
apparently did not occur to me. Besides, I had decided
that I must be dependent on alcohol to overcome my
conditioned shyness around girls. The stuff had been
advertised as social lubricant, and that sounded not just

useful but flat-out necessary. It would be strategically ridiculous to approach a girl I liked without such a basic preparatory tactic. But aside from my joyless, calculated partying, I made no attempt to update my technique of failing to approach women. I assured myself that my new, painstakingly carefree attitude in social situations, combined with my new environment and binge drinking, would be enough to woo a mate.

The results were mixed. Often I was alone at the end of the party, casting out woozy come-hither looks at anything with vaguely compatible chromosomes, and then at two fifteen I'd return, wasted, to an empty bed. Perhaps the only proven, consistently effective pickup technique I picked up was two words, *David* and *Bowie*. I'd first encountered the thin white bastard's music at the end of my senior year of high school, when a friend recommended *Ziggy Stardust*. I quickly ran through the rest of his catalog, and as a demonstration of my fandom I purchased a shrunken, fake-vintage T-shirt printed with the cover of *Aladdin Sane*. People are apparently very, very impressed by David Bowie. Men would nod at him approvingly; women swooned and occasionally reached with reverent hands to brush his silkscreen face. This baffled me. Everyone understood, intuitively, that David Bowie was awesome, but it apparently never occurred to anyone else to listen to his music or to buy a shirt with his horrible bony face. By wearing his visage

and sometimes talking about his albums I quite accidentally became his disciple, an initiate of the diamond
dogma, born again as a spider from Mars. It was the fe-
tishization of indie music pushed to an erotic extreme.
*You apparently have at least some familiarity with a popular
musician who recorded most of his music before I was born. This
qualifies you as an acceptable mate. Come, let us make out now.*

So yes, every once in a while a girl would respond to
my manly wilting. This always took a little time, since
verbalization was forbidden, but using my teary, intoxicated eyes for strategic undressings I sometimes managed
to convey my incredibly specific, frequently reprehensible plans. On these rare evenings we would return to
someone's dorm room together and skip through increasingly intimate behaviors. But the interplay of my
Catholic guilt and my alcohol consumption (each encouraging the other) usually left me paralyzed before
anything irreversible happened. Sometimes I would go
home with the same young lady more than once con-
secutively, or visit her in her dorm room on a Sunday
afternoon, and we called this "dating." This happened
rarely, and never lasted very long.

My restraint finally failed me one Friday night, in
the spring of my freshman year. Impossibly and perfectly
it was the Friday before Easter Sunday, it was Good Friday when the thing happened. I went home with a girl
I did not know. In an alcoholic swoon, the arbitrary

line I had drawn as a boundary for my sexual activity blurred and then vanished entirely. My virginity was lost in the most literal sense; it was misplaced, I swear, I took my eyes off of it for a sec but just a sec and then it was gone. The act was so brief, so joyless, so spectacularly unmemorable that I am certain it will be seared into my consciousness until I die.

I did not attend Mass that Sunday morning, but even outside of church I was fossilized by my guilt; so as a secular humanist alternative to Sunday services I decided to go for a walk in the woods and have a casual, meditative chat with my Creator. I expressed contrition and confusion. Could I be forgiven for a meaningless indulgence, a mistake that caused harm mainly in that it provided me with an opportunity for extensive self-flagellation? Or would the Lord condemn me because I had failed to express my self-disgust that morning in an officially approved manner? I asked for a sign.

We have now arrived at one of those instances for which I am perversely grateful for autobiography. We have reached an incident of such astounding coincidence and hackneyed, blatant symbolism that it would be completely implausible in a work of fiction. But I can use it here because, cross my heart and hope to die, it actually happened. As consolation to the skeptical reader, I was also entirely aware at the time of the seemingly contrived nature of the incident, which is part of the reason it was so terrifying. It seemed exactly like the sort of thing someone would make up.

So. As I was leaving the forest that afternoon, I happened to pass by a creek. It was early spring, after a long and dry winter, and although a thin trickle of water ran down the middle of the riverbed it was still mostly mud. In one cloudy puddle I noticed a bunch of frogs. They sat, and croaked at each other, and then without foreplay or forewarning one suddenly mounted another; although I am not an expert on amphibian anatomy it appeared that the female climbed on top of the male. The two animals proceeded to fuck, vigorously and joylessly, as I watched, horrified.

At this point a hairy old man, hiking the campus alone, noticed me from the path and walked over to see what I was staring at. It did not take him long to notice the frogs as well. "Boy," he leered, amused and a little astounded. "They're really going at it, aren't they?"

Reflecting on the hideous mechanical nature of the reproductive act, accompanied by this creepy husk of a person, I noticed a snake coiling itself around a root near the edge of the puddle. It secured itself to the shore and, once steady, struck forward and sank its fangs deep into the thigh of the male frog. The frog immediately stopped moving (I assume paralyzed by toxins and the sheer agony of the bite), while the female kept on humping as if nothing had happened. The snake, meanwhile, had unhinged its jaw and was proceeding to swallow whole its still-fucking prey.

In retrospect I find it remarkable that I did not leave college immediately to enter the seminary.

Thus my first academic year of romantic activity ended, alternately boring and traumatic. I had some guilty Catholic sex, I had some sexy Catholic guilt. In the end, having participated for the first time in any number of horrible activities, I was no wiser about love and relationships than I had been when I started. And even as I dealt with life at college, my symptoms had not disappeared entirely. The bad thoughts recurred sporadically, like heat lightning against a summer sky, like motion and then a thread of crimson beneath still water. There were signs and symbols and I, concerned with a thousand other things, cheerfully ignored them. Each time the symptoms returned I suffered briefly, but when they eventually subsided I told myself that they had gone forever, that I had turned a corner and that I could finally enjoy the wonderful future I had been promised. That everything would be better, not just after but forever after.

As my classes ended and my symptoms quietly escalated, I swore that next year I would at last find a meaningful relationship. I had experienced minor turbulence adjusting to college, of course, but this was to be expected, and as a wise and world-weary sophomore I expected my next academic year to be triumphant. I would undo those months of shame and loneliness by digging up someone whom I could safely adore. I was determined to spend the summer refining myself, exercising and studying, becoming a more confident and attractive person. And then I would return, and I would fall in love. Everything would be different.

I had no idea. I had absolutely no idea.

6

Mad Love

I returned from college to find my home comfortably unchanged. As we pulled into the driveway Bear leaped and howled at the door, behavior that had been endearing when he was a puppy but that now threatened the structural integrity of our home's framework. I went to my room to find Moonbeam, terrified by the dog's barking, hiding under the covers of my bed. He greeted me with affection before he remembered that he was obligated to ignore me and sauntered away badass, tail twitching. My sister was several weeks away from finishing her second year of high school. My father was still involved in public practice and my mother was directing a bank and both were still capable of reducing me, quite unintentionally, to a quivering lump of guilt and self-loathing with a single disapproving word. It was good to be home.

Although not spectacularly happy, I was generally satisfied with my circumstances, and because of this I decided it was finally time to scale back my psychological treatment. I told the pill-vending golem that was my hypothetical psychiatrist that I was ready to stop the medication. There was a brief meeting, a gesture of mechanical assent, and I was given a timetable over which to intermittently decrease my intake of Effexor.

This decision was intended as a final demonstration of confidence in my supposed recovery. Yet I find the whole business highly suspicious in retrospect. It was as if, subconsciously recognizing the slow return of my madness, I discontinued treatment in order to prove to myself that it was not actually a problem. If I was sick I would be taking medicine. If I wasn't taking medicine, I could not be sick.

I spent that summer working at the Harvard Coop. The bookstore began as a school cooperative, and as is the way of such things it was eventually bought out by a parking-lot book-chain behemoth, although this did not stop the management from continuing to make proud and meaningless claims of financial independence. The store thus became an unfortunate hybrid, providing the cold corporate indifference and administrative incompetence of a chain, along with the mediocre selection and clueless salesmanship of a local mom-and-popper. Many of our patrons were either the local homeless, on the verge of heatstroke and collapsed in smelly piles at the store café, or tourists looking for T-shirts and public bathrooms. Neither demographic demonstrated special appreciation for the printed word.

I am vaguely embarrassed at the naïve enthusiasm with which I originally approached this position: I liked books, and the place sold books, and presumably there was some way to make this work. Sadly, university book retail was a poor match for me. I officially began my literary career distributing caps and gowns for Harvard's graduate school graduation. At first I experienced tremendous guilt, overcharging our clientele hundreds of dollars for the six-hour rental of a large wearable blanket: a garment of such poor quality that it would begin to hemorrhage purple dye at the slightest touch of humidity. But my conscience was eased by the fact that my customers were graduating from Harvard, and so they were probably very wealthy and also terrible people. The graduates obliged me by confirming my stereotypes. They arrived to collect their rental gowns either belligerent or drunk, and would frequently attempt to date my female coworkers. It is a truism in retail that you will slowly begin to hate your customers, and the future alumni of the institution did much to aid this process.

After the graduation ceremonies ended I was transferred to the children's section, which, needless to say, demonstrated a questionable distribution of human resources. Corralling small and irritable children is not necessarily a talent of mine. I like kids just fine, but I was trying to grow a beard, and my voice has always registered at frequencies audible only to whales. Basically, young children find me terrifying and they do not listen to me. My apparent generational disconnect with the swinging young people of today did not help, either. I might observe a customer paging through a trashy gossip-girl novel and recommend a Caldecott award winner instead. "Let me get this straight," she'd reply. "I can read my book, which is essentially pornography, or I can read your book about the boy with shoes." "*Magic* shoes," I would reply. "He fights racism!" The results were predictable.

When I was not bothering children I was marooned on the fiction level, left utterly without work, hovering like a vulture over browsing customers in hopes that they might abandon their products and give me something to do; a mis-shelved copy of *Life of Pi* thus became a seismic event, a flash of interest amid the tedium. I remember disposing of countless damaged copies of

Wicked, the die-cut circular window in the cover torn during shipping. I remember eyeing scrawny, quasi-adolescent customers who would park themselves at the café for hours without buying anything but leave neat piles of Japanese manga like scat. I logged into the inventory system for the sole purpose of reading archived reviews of embarrassing novels by former child actors. I spoke on the phone with lonely old women so desperate for conversation that they had taken to dialing up random bored employees at franchise bookstores; and then at the earliest opportunity I politely and callously ended the conversation so that I could return to my crucial task of reordering the opus of Chuck Palahniuk by date of publication. And every night, before I went home, I was forced to wait for the head of security to conduct a search of my person; and every night there was an uncomfortable exchange as I explained to him that I had brought my own copy of David Foster Wallace's *Infinite Jest,* that I was not stealing an identical copy each day as part of an elaborate heist that required huge blocks of stolen postmodern literature, presumably to outfit my henchmen with bludgeoning weapons.

As I lurched zombielike around the bookstore, the OCD took endless pleasure in tormenting my poor unoccupied brain, like a child pulling legs from a fly. I was off the medication again and the bad thoughts had started to return, although I still tried to deny their existence. I spent much of that summer packing up and shipping back titles from small Christian publishers, ruminating on exactly how thoroughly and succulently I would be roasted in hell. At other times an innocent passerby would trigger a sudden spurt of graphic imagery. It was an unpleasant experience and I still hold a great deal of bitterness toward my former employer. Indeed, I have to admit that one of my few pleasures during my eventual hospitalization was my father's endearingly lame suggestion that when I left my job for the hospital I had (yuk yuk) flown the Coop. One flew east, one flew west, one flew over . . . you know the rest.

I finally returned to Swarthmore in late August, to write and act in the orientation play. A Pennsylvania summer is a terrible thing. The sidewalks are wet and smell foul, and are covered with the crisp shiny carcasses of giant beetles. At any moment you might hear a sudden hum and then a cicada would fly at your head like a crunchy wet bullet. My mother drove me to campus in the sweltering heat, and we moved my belongings into a cavernous quad at the edge of campus. These living conditions were not ideal, but I brainstormed creative and idiotic solutions. In the absence of an actual window screen, for example, I decided to take two of the collapsible screens provided and attach them to the building with duct tape. Similarly, while I was disappointed that I did not have my own single, I decided I might move my bed into a huge walk-in closet set off from the main room; fortunately, the school had left an enormous, useless metal cabinet inside the closet. The rusty monolith proved impossible to budge and it scraped open my unprotected sandaled foot when I tried to move it. Thus I began my sophomore year of college aggravated and overheated, beset by insects, an ugly mash of flesh and nail and tetanus where my big toe should have been. After we called the hospital and determined that I was not at significant risk of contracting the lockjaw, my mother told me she loved me and then drove away—ruminating, I assume, on the cost of my tuition and the unusual duration of her pregnancy with me.

The freshman orientation play is a Swarthmore College tradition. It was conceived on the principle that the best way to teach terrified, annoyed children about the boring fundamentals of college life is to parade their otherwise-intimidating elders around in grotesque spectacle. We wore silly outfits, we sang an acoustic ballad about proper condom use and we hilariously feigned the effects of alcohol poisoning, all in the name of edutainment. I spent those first weeks catching up with friends and playing videogames constantly to silence the voices in my head, and practicing a lame New Jersey accent. (I was—inexplicably, considering my lack of experience with nonprescription pharmaceuticals—cast in the play as the badass stoner kid. Somewhere in the darkest corner of my dresser there is still an undershirt decorated with a giant iron-on pot leaf. I think I was supposed to return it to the costume shop. If anyone in the Swarthmore drama department would like to claim it, please e-mail me.)

I have tried to postpone it but eventually I'll have to write about The Girl, capital Tee and capital Gee. There are many things that I would like to say about The Girl. I could probably waste my life cataloging the minutiae of our relationship, filling weighty hardbacks with dense nostalgic prose in French for some reason until I die. Understand that she was the first girl I really loved, and who to all appearances loved me back—not in a healthy way, not at all, but for the first time one of my creepy fixations was reciprocated with equivalent pathology. I will keep this chapter as short as possible, so as not to test my audience's patience, nor to pour creative salt into fresh and extremely fucking painful psychosexual wounds.

The Girl was beautiful. I am not trying to aggrandize my hypothetical mack; during sophomore year my seduction technique, as it were, involved staring down attractive women without blinking and repeating to myself, again and again, "I am nineteen-seventies hairy-chested love-god Batman." I was floppy-haired, lanky, confused, and self-conscious. I grew a scruffy goatee because it was the only symmetrical, continuous pattern of facial hair I could produce.

But The Girl attended Bryn Mawr, and Bryn Mawr students were not known for sophisticated seduction strategies. Bryn Mawr is a women's liberal arts college near Swarthmore. It was the third member of the suburban Pennsylvania academic consortium that also included Swarthmore and Haverford; regular shuttles ran between the schools, encouraging students to visit the other institutions for academic enrichment and Quaker eugenics. Of course we never had time to visit the other schools, and instead we developed vicious unfounded stereotypes about the unseen inhabitants of our sibling institutions. I heard occasional rumors that Haverford students had their faces on their chests, and ate the flesh of men. But more popular was the perception that Haverford, shamefully ranking only tenth out of the dozens of institutions rated by *U.S. News & World Report,* was the Dumb One (as of this writing Swarthmore is ranked third). I've discussed Swarthmore's propensity for self-stereotyping at length, and Haverford was regarded with fondness and affection by Swarthmore students because it provided us with a way to contextualize our self-loathing. We took tremendous comfort in our superficial ugliness and our wretched, curdled little souls; we thus came to view Haverford students as the cute and popular majority (actual size of each student body is irrelevant) who enabled our dejected underdog status. We imagined them excluding us, and we publicly mocked their superficial, judgmental attitudes, yet we were secretly grateful that the pretext of their disapproval allowed us to refine our self-criticism further. We hated Haverford, inasmuch as it allowed us to hate ourselves more efficiently and coherently. I believe that actual Haverford students, in contrast, knew Swarthmore only as a place that sometimes threw giant sex parties, and that had a pretty lame Division III lacrosse team.

But Bryn Mawr. Bryn Mawr students had something of a reputation; if you hung around any Swarthmore party long enough you would inevitably hear complaints about the bryn-mawr-gurls. This was said very quickly, as if one long word, such was its ubiquity in the Swarthmore idiom. The labeling was not entirely unfounded. The extreme conditions of life at Bryn Mawr College (stress, intellectual stimulation, astronomical estrogen levels, near-constant aggravation of normal but ordinarily repressed bisexual tendencies) had predictable effects on its student body. Although some were content on their own campus, countless others would flock to Swarthmore on weekend evenings to partake of our renowned party scene, if by "renowned" one means "had some boys." If you waited in the health center parking lot around nine o'clock on a Friday night, you would observe a slew of them arrive on the tri-co van, desperate for nerd love and deep in flame, stumbling forth from the bus and making lewd suggestions toward anything with fewer than two X chromosomes. They had been psychologically rewired, perceiving the world in duotone terminator vision, constantly scanning and running sexy diagnostics on potential targets.

For what it's worth, the relationship between Bryn Mawr and Swarthmore ran both ways. Bryn Mawr Halloween parties were the stuff of salacious legend, and it was not uncommon on a Halloween night for clusters of Swarthmore boys, curiosity ignited by drink and stoked by sugar, to make an impromptu pilgrimage to the beloved sister school. I went once, while dating The Girl. I cannot imagine any sight more dispiriting than that Sunday-morning ride back to Swarthmore: the van filled to capacity with disheveled batmen and remorseful ninja turtles, shells crooked and marked with unidentifiable stains.

I realize that I am toeing the precipice of accidental misogyny in my descriptions. By the same token, some of you will be uncomfortable with my unflattering depiction of The Girl through the rest of this chapter. The generic alias I've chosen for her suggests a hornet's nest of gender issues. I believe that if I had invented The Girl myself and presented her here as a plausible fictional character, I would probably (and quite rightly) be criticized. So please believe that I know that The Girl is implausible. She is only real, and I am committed to telling about our relationship as I experienced it, through the eyes of a naïve and deeply troubled boy. I cannot re-create her perspective, and to imagine it in the context of this memoir would be unfair to both of us. So consider yourself warned that I have reduced a complicated and troubled young woman to a shallow, life-denying, borderline-sociopathic harpy. Other than that, I can only repeat my refrain: Please do not criticize me excessively, because I tried to kill myself before and may again.

I had decided that fall to take a course on Vladimir Nabokov at Bryn Mawr. My only previous experience with bryn-mawr-gurls had occurred early in my freshman year when, thanks to a spectacularly contrived series of miscommunications worthy of a network situation comedy, a young lady had not entirely accidentally missed her bus and then arranged to spend the night with my roommate. He wasn't interested, however, and the poor girl spent the night in a sleeping bag on our floor getting trampled whenever I got up to go to the bathroom. So that fall our young hero was anticipating, somewhat nervously, not only studying one of the great authors of the twentieth century but also being mobbed by legions of sex-crazed nymphomaniac amazon undergrads. Needless to say, one of these expectations would not be met.

Instead, amid the nervous BMC girls and the slumming Haverford kids, I noticed The Girl. She was difficult not to notice. She was pale and slender, with sandy hair and sharp, thoughtful eyes. I introduced myself to her, uneasily, and each of us spent the duration of our first lesson failing to notice the other's unceasing stare. After the class ended I wondered aloud, not entirely innocently, if someone could help me find the registrar. I was then taken down like a wounded antelope. She ran me down, sliced open my hindquarters, snapped away the circling buzzards, and then waited for me to pass out from blood loss. We had lunch the following day, and then again on Friday, at a sandwich franchise off of Bryn Mawr's campus.

These meals were cute but uneventful. We talked. She smoked her cigarettes, and kept her eyes half shut, and smiled at me intermittently. At one point I dropped a slice of cucumber on her foot and sort of felt like an asshole. But then fortune smiled upon me: A friend called, cuing up a harsh distorted midi of David Bowie's "Rebel Rebel" from my cell phone. I tugged the phone from my pocket and apologetically silenced it, but the necessary information had been conveyed.

"You like David Bowie?" she asked, intrigued.

"Yes," I replied, with tremendous confidence and barely concealed relief. Because even in the edgy atmosphere of our second date I could still, if nothing else, declare with absolute certainty that I liked David Bowie. If asked I could provide an extensive portfolio of evidence supporting this. But I was told this was unnecessary, and was invited to watch a movie with her that night.

The Girl really was beautiful, objectively, like seriously ten out of ten. I was nineteen, and I'd never been in love before, and I was pretty much utterly fucking besotted. She liked comic books and she wore black nail polish and she played Super Nintendo RPGs on her computer. She wore glasses, fer Chrissakes, legitimate sexy-librarian-style glasses. She was tall but not too tall, slender, had auburn hair and freckles that only really showed when she was tired or embarrassed. She was brilliant and funny and insightful, and she was crazy about me, and she suffered from untreated depression and anorexia and self-mutilation and obsessive-compulsive disorder.

Somewhere, against the ring of debris encircling a giant gas planet, God struck a single cosmic rim shot.

Our movie date was postponed when, due to unnecessary preparations on my part, I missed the shuttle from Swat to Bryn. I still wince a little at the memory of that evening, sprinting in shorts, my hair and sandals alike flip-flopping absurdly as I shouted and jogged. I can imagine the bus driver, watching my pathetic dash and immediately deducing my situation, and then sadistically driving on with a cruel chuckle. I cannot say I blame him. Such absolute power to cockblock must swiftly corrupt. Anyway, the Girl and I rescheduled, and the following evening I succeeded in navigating the tri-co van schedule. I would come to know this van well over the course of the semester. The commute took between twenty minutes and half an hour, and I was always sure to bring a textbook, yet despite my most well-intentioned efforts I was never able to finish much homework on the bus. This was not due to my fellow passengers, who were generally quiet and immobile, with the exception of Friday night ladies with sketchy intent. No, my problem was with the van driver, who played dire Philadelphia radio stations, oscillating between R & B and adult contemporary, at inexcusable volume. I quickly learned to take the second row of seats from the back, which was farthest from any single set of speakers, but nonetheless I was often forced to increase my headphones' volume to unhealthy levels preemptively. Aside from the psychological damage I suffered that semester, I don't think my hearing will ever recover.

The Girl greeted me that evening with a nervous hug and then brought me to her room. She had a small, neat single in a dorm near the snack bar, vastly preferable to my own cavernous residence. The first sign of trouble was when, surveying her posters of fourteenth-century apocalyptic art and her impressive library, I noticed a pair of handcuffs dangling from her desk lamp. When asked, she chuckled nervously and told me that these were a (professional-quality, presumably very expensive) gag gift. I did not pursue the subject. Second sign: She chose from her DVD collection *Quills*, a biopic of the Marquis de Sade that prominently features its leading man's naked ass. This was also a little unnerving but I remained confident that everything was perfect and wonderful. Then the third sign: After an hour or so of us watching French costume-drama fucking, after we kissed for the first time, she rolled up her sleeve and told me she didn't feel right keeping this from me any longer and showed me a series of short horizontal scabs across her forearm.

The powers that be were punking me again. I am not a gifted comedian, but I can still recognize classic joke structure. Two beats and then the punch line.

It is impossible to mistake the scars left by cutting for any other type of injury. After one has been identified for you, you will never fail to recognize another. An actor in a local play, or a cashier at a supermarket—suddenly the nondescript scratches across their skin become signifiers of pain, harbingers of undesired intimacy with a troubled stranger. She hands you your groceries and tells you to "have a nice day" while she bears, scarred into her flesh, marks that signify overwhelming suffering. And while she smiles you cannot help but wonder what that face looks like scowling and sobbing in agony, what those clean hands would look like clutching a razor, sticky with blood.

As the wounds scar, they become soft and pale, tiny raised lines parallel against the skin. They possess unique significance, an unmistakable language. I am not referring to troubled individuals who cut words or symbols into their arms. Even the most basic self-injuries possess disturbing regularity. They are deliberate, exact. Over time the wounds form patterns, they speak to one another. They tell a story. You cannot mistake them for any accidental cut or scrape because the world for all its cruelty never injures us with such precision. They are the kind of injury that can be inflicted only upon the self.

The Girl said that she was better now, and although I observed that several of her wounds were still fresh I believed her. At the time I saw her suicidal tendencies as another common interest, like how we were both vegetarians and we both loved videogames. We had been sick, but neither of us was sick anymore. It was just something else we had in common. I put an arm around her shoulder, and she kissed me.

So we started dating. And it did not take the disorder long to realize that The Girl could be used as a weapon against me. I believed that I loved her, and I managed to wait about five days before I told her as much; but the moment I communicated these feelings the disorder began to voice objections. Can you be certain, it asked, that you love her? That you are not lying? That you are not trying to hurt her, hurt the person whom you care most about right now, hurt her in literal, terrible ways, and from here to crueler suggestions you are sick and in denial and worse and worse again. I grappled with it, tried to silence it, but it was a debate I could not win. I could never demonstrate my feelings strongly enough to silence the disorder, and the more I struggled the more complicated my actual feelings became. It is difficult to love when one's emotions are entangled in escalating, circular madness. I remember the first time she admitted she returned my feelings, and experiencing a little jolt of warmth and excitement in my chest. It was a sensation I immediately isolated, sterilized, and documented, taking care to avoid the possibility of contamination. I would attempt to use this fleeting moment of actual feeling as evidence in later dialogues with the voices. *She loves me,* I told myself with feigned astonishment and rising nausea. *She said she loves me.* But of course I wasn't really talking to myself.

In light of our mutual vulnerability we agreed early on to "take things slow." Physically, this meant that we managed to remain chaste for about two weeks, our mutual appetites barely sated by a routine of kissing and frenzied, irregular writhing against each other. Then at one point (about twenty minutes before our third Nabokov class, if I remember correctly) a stray hand might have brushed a bra clasp, and soon after the Thing Was Done. It was all right. She was demanding, and I inexperienced, but we worked things out okay. Foolishly, I agreed to intercourse without protection. I told her that I preferred to use condoms, on general principle, but she reassured me that she was on the pill, and we decided that in a relationship as dependable and deeply felt as ours we could trust each other not to transmit infections. The miraculous antibiotic power of our love would protect against disease. Looking back, our exact logic escapes me, although as befuddled mentally ill nineteen-year-olds I'm sure the argument was sound.

Still, she was sympathetic to my sexual anxieties, which I blamed on my latent Catholic tendencies. Much, much later I would find out that her father was himself a bitter and guilt-stricken former Catholic, and that she had not informed me of this at the time because she "didn't want to freak me out." This would become a recurring theme over the course of our relationship: her knowing about things she really, probably should have told me, and then not telling me because she "didn't want to freak me out."

She was right, of course, that many of her little tidbits would have upset me, although I do not think my distress would have been unjustified.

For example, she also told me that because she was taking birth control pills she no longer had her period. Looking back, it should have been suspicious that in such a hotbed of estrogen she was somehow magically able to eliminate her menstrual cycle. She had told me she was no longer anorexic, and I believed her, and at no point did it occur to me that her eating disorder might have been what was interfering with her periods.

We practiced equal delicacy and restraint in developing emotional intimacy. We agreed, in an embarrassingly earnest moment of commitment, not to discuss marriage seriously until after graduation. This did not stop us from talking about baby names. It was through these conversations about our family that we conceived of Morrissey, a hypothetical child who combined our worst attributes. Morrissey was brilliant but superior and condescending; when The Girl imitated him she would speak in a nasal, effeminate voice. We laughed a great deal about Morrissey, but both of us understood that after so many jokes we could never give the name to our actual child. Vladimir: This was the name I decided on, in honor of Nabokov, without whom we could never have met. Vladimir. This was the name I wanted for the child we would have after our wedding, after my wedding to the girl who wanted to die. These conversations did not strike either of us unusual or presumptuous.

"You're crazy," I said, teasing, trying to suggest that I could barely hide my infatuation.

"Crazy in love!" was the blushing response, sentimental and knowingly silly, embarrassed as she said it but saying it anyway.

A month after we started dating I bought her a stuffed toy of Cthulhu, the extraterrestrial demon from the horror stories of H. P. Lovecraft. For the uninitiated, Cthulhu is a gigantic winged motherfucker with an octopus for a head, and although he is currently entombed at the bottom of the Pacific he has ambitious long-term goals related to eating the planet. In retrospect, the fact that this adorable plush approximation of an undead harbinger of despair was deemed to be an appropriate representation of our love might have indicated that something was wrong. For what it's worth she loved the damned thing. And anyways everything was wonderful. We loved each other. We talked and laughed and went out for smoothies together. We ate meals at the Bryn Mawr dining hall because she always seemed to have extra meals available for me to use, somehow, and while I ate heartily she seemed content to pick at egg whites and bits of salad; while I was oblivious at the time, looking back I am aghast that I so eagerly consumed the food that she should have been eating. The Girl and I played videogames together and we walked together to the comic book store. She cut herself only occasionally.

I remember waiting in the Bryn Mawr student health center for her one afternoon. She emerged from the appointment irate. With a grotesque parody of an Indian accent, in imitation of her psychiatrist, she told me that the woman had refused to prescribe her less than two weeks of medication at a time. The Girl was pissed, because The Girl was convinced if she was entrusted with so many pills all at once she might use them to try to kill herself. I asked why The Girl didn't tell the psychiatrist this and The Girl explained that she resented any professional intrusion into her privacy. I offered to hold on to the surplus medication for her. She thanked me for being concerned but said she didn't want to get me involved in her problems.

So because she hated talking to therapists I got to be Doctor Boyfriend. Each time she crumpled I gave her insipid advice, and I held her, and we told each other everything was fine. This was my responsibility. I loved her. My disorder took note of my unhappiness and my growing ambivalence, and try as I might it would never quite let me forget them. But I could not leave her. I had made a commitment to her from which I could not back down, and I was determined to save her even if it killed us both. None of this was unusual or inappropriate. This was how a relationship worked. We loved each other. And besides, neither of us was sick anymore, not really.

I cannot be the only young person who, boggled by innocence and a lifetime of bad fantasy, throws himself selflessly into a damned and damning romance. You probably won't listen, as I didn't listen, but I am obliged to say it anyway: You cannot save them. You cannot fix them. Love does not conquer all; love can become a parasite, if you let it, it can allow two lives to be destroyed instead of one. Sometimes love doesn't mean shit.

I remember the precise moment when I felt our relationship begin to strain. It was over fall break. I had returned home to Boston, and set about irritating my parents and sister with unceasing fawning and simpering over The Girl. I talked to her, every day, for at least half an hour; I think something around 42 minutes was my record, as I carefully noted the duration of each conversation in an attempt to challenge my disorder's insinuations about the relationship. I remember quite distinctly talking with her, locked in the upstairs bathroom for privacy, walking in circles, and climbing up on the tub as we spoke. We were talking about videogames. I was playing Resident Evil 4 at the time, a politically insensitive and endearingly dumb action game in which an American supercop slaughters entire villages of rural Spanish quasi-zombies. The conversation eventually turned to the two-player fighting game Marvel vs. Capcom, a title we both had some affection for. Marvel vs. Capcom allows the player to pit the Incredible Hulk against Mega Man and generic ninja-types among many, many pretty flashing lights and colors, a spectacle surpassed only by Nintendo's Super Smash Bros. series. We had talked about the game before, and were talking about it again, we were devoting a lengthy chunk of our conversation exclusively to this game. And it became apparent to me then that we could not stop talking about the game; if we tried to discuss anything of substance she would be forced to talk about her suffering, and I about my frustration with my utter helplessness. So instead we talked about the game, about how you could make Spider-Man fight Chun-Li, and how awesome that was. We talked about the game. We talked about the game.

When I returned from break, right after I arrived on campus, I received a phone call from The Girl. Travel was always difficult for her, although she told me that taking antianxiety medication or coercing a glass of wine from the flight attendant was usually enough to calm her. That afternoon, lacking immediate access to appropriate substances, she had begun to lose herself. She was at the 30th Street train station in Philadelphia, she told me, and surrounded by crowds. She had started to panic. She wanted quite desperately to kill herself. She needed to see me. I agreed to meet her at Bryn Mawr and immediately checked the Swarthmore Web site only to find that intercollegiate van services had yet to resume, and then found a regional train schedule. I might be able to see her that night, I told her, but the trip would take several hours and would cost something like $15 (a significant expense for a college student). I would then need to spend the rest of the night in her room, and this was always difficult because she was taking sleeping medication, and while unconscious she would sometimes lash out or scream. But I told her I would come to her, if she needed me. I offered to do this, cognizant of the fact that it was unreasonable and insane, because I was sure she would decline. I paused as I awaited her refusal. She was silent for a moment and then spoke. That would be nice, she said, her voice a little brighter now, bleak but coy and almost flirtatious. She said that she wanted to see me. After long minutes and a panicked call to my parents, I called her back and apologetically retracted my offer. Writing this out now I am struck by the cruelty and the absurdity of the situation. It was not something I was psychologically equipped to deal with. I was being asked to spend time and resources I did not have, to rescue someone I cared about deeply from terrible pain.

Because I was really all that she had at this point. I cannot claim to have ever been much of a debutante, but I had a small and steady circle of friends at Swarthmore. I had my comedy group and friends from my freshman hall. Yet by this time in the semester The Girl had drawn back into borderline hermitage. I might occasionally tell her a story or a joke I'd heard from a friend; all of her stories were about conversations with her mother or her younger brother, or were about funny videos that she had seen online. It does not seem unreasonable to guess that The Girl suffered from acute social anxiety. Once, I invited her to dinner with my friends from my hall, and the entire time she sat petrified, her smile queasy and saccharine. Although I would not admit it to myself at the time I remember experiencing feelings of panic and vague embarrassment, as if I had promised to show them a new puppy and they decided it was ugly, or as if I were an ambitious stage parent whose child succeeded only at wetting itself and crying for the cameras. She, for her part, was aware of my scrutiny and was paralyzed by it. The only time she actually moved or said anything was when an acquaintance said something insulting about smokers, and The Girl triumphantly produced her cigarette lighter from her purse. She smiled proudly, pleased about taking the opportunity to self-deprecate. Jubilant to have made some kind of contribution to the conversation, however tangential and self-negating.

She never made much of an impression on my friends. Some of them chuckled knowingly when I told them about her, and some of them when I showed them pictures remarked that she was, in fact, pretty hot. But, not wanting to violate her privacy, I never did more than hint about our troubles. Late one night after a party a perpetually single friend of mine told me, with a slight pang of bitterness, how beautiful The Girl was, and how lucky I was to have her. I agreed, although I mentioned that things were not going well for us at the moment, as she was dealing with some personal problems. He nodded. Then he told me that the important thing was to be there for her, and to do everything I could to help her deal with whatever it was. I took his advice to heart. Occasionally, others whom I considered friends were impossibly, thoughtlessly cruel. One acquaintance observed how The Girl looked sort of "emo," and jokingly wondered if she'd ever tried to cut herself. I told The Girl about this later, and we laughed and laughed and laughed, because I don't think either of us was capable of any other response.

Another time, later in the semester, she came over to see a performance by my sketch comedy troupe. I'd encouraged her to sit with some of my roommates, so she wouldn't be alone, but while I quickly located my friends in the back of the audience I could not find her. It was only after the first sketch had ended that I peeked out from backstage and noticed her, several rows in, sitting alone. She was beaming at me. I don't think I once observed her break her gaze, over the course of the entire show; I might have been sitting in the background picking my nose in one scene and still she stared, transfixed, radiating love and devotion completely incommensurate with our actual relationship. I took her to the cast party that night and she was content to huddle on my lap, steadily drinking, wincing behind a boozy smile when anyone other than me tried to talk to her.

She left early that night to take the van home, but a few minutes after she said good-bye she stomped back in, despondent. She had missed the bus, she told me. Unaware of why this would be a problem I told her not to worry, that another van would be there in an hour or two, placed my fingers up to her face, and tried gently to press her mouth into a smile. She slapped my hands away with surprising violence. I understand, now, the futility of my gesture, how condescending and cruel it must have seemed. The party, like any strange social environment, was anathema to her. She must have been in agony from the moment she entered the room. But that evening I was baffled by her response. We left the party and returned to my room, both a little drunk. I wasted time on my computer and she curled up on my bed, unmoving although not necessarily asleep. After an hour or so I shook her and we walked over to the bus, which took her home.

We never fought again after that party. I think she recognized that night how utterly dependent upon me she was, and so became determined not to alienate her last human contact in an increasingly hostile world. For my part, while I was steadily growing more irritated with her passivity, I remained meek around her. I was terrified of hurting her, whatever "hurt" meant in this context.

In spite of increasing dysfunction, we made countless efforts to convince ourselves we were stable. One of the most amusing incidents occurred one afternoon when I demanded she dispose of the special box of sterilized razors she kept for self-mutilation. We walked to a nearby pond and tossed them in. They made a satisfying plop as they broke the surface. This was tremendously meaningful, and also symbolic, and presumably representative of some new corner or pathway that our relationship had enabled her to turn upon. We held hands and hugged and were generally very pleased with ourselves. Of course, disposing of the razors was treating not the disease but a symptom, in the most superficial and obnoxious way possible. No amount of sharpened metal submerged and left to rust would have made her healthy. If she had been an alcoholic we probably would have tossed in a flask instead, as if this represented the global supply of alcohol, as if once the single object of her temptation was disposed of she would never again be troubled. It was shameful. It was an after-school special, a made-for-television solution, applied to a problem that demanded infinitely greater sophistication and commitment to resolve. To be fair, I do not recall her again cutting her wrists, although I suspect her subsequent fascination with corset piercings may not have been entirely coincidental. I recall her explaining the procedure to me and then removing her shirt to show me her stitched-up back, like a kinky human voodoo doll. If I had reservations I chose not to express them.

We were no longer having actual conversations. It was all cruel monotony. We didn't talk any more really, just regurgitated past dialogues about nothing, comics, and online and bullshit; repeating ourselves on ever-quickening cycles, feigning light and savvy banter together in agony. Nintendo-Marvel-Marvel-Lovecraft, and then interminable moments of horrible silence and then around to Nintendo again. We would eat in the cafeteria and have conversations without substance, she only picking at salad and egg whites, and then we would return to her room and have ugly, mechanical sex. As she increased her medication her libido dropped accordingly, and these dull, brief encounters became shorter and less frequent, although neither of us really cared.

I discussed all of this with my Swarthmore therapist, explaining in embarrassing detail my neuroses surrounding the collapsing relationship. For months, while I stubbornly kept claiming that I was in love with The Girl, I gradually revealed to my therapist the whole toxic, dysfunctional mess. Although I am not sure that she grasped the severity of our situation, to her credit she seemed at least mildly concerned. When I described The Girl's refusal to see a psychologist, for example, the therapist would nod and agree that it sounded like The Girl might benefit from some psychological counseling. She clearly did not recognize the extremely dangerous aspects of the relationship, for both her own patient and another equally troubled young person. If she did, and if she sincerely believed that her occasional gentle suggestions would be enough, then whatever her intentions were she was wrong. Her response was analogous to, had I been an alcoholic, leaving me locked up alone with a case of beer and a handle of vodka. I had assembled the mechanism that would enable my destruction, and although she was not technically responsible for this, in some ways her gentle concern did far more harm than actual malice ever could have. Had she somehow actively fucked up, I might have sought treatment somewhere else. But without reason to distrust her I was content to continue working together. I was being counseled, so there was nothing more I could do. Everything was fine.

Late in the semester The Girl and I exchanged Christmas gifts. I cannot recall what I got her, but she presented me with a large bulky package that contained a stuffed Cthulhu, much like the one I'd bought for her several months back. This one, however, was inexplicably and idiotically dressed as a superhero. The utter improbability that such an object, cult horror inelegantly mashed up with popular heroic fantasy, would actually be produced and marketed was staggering. For a moment I wondered who would be inspired to purchase such a horrible fucking thing, and for whom. But The Girl bought one, for me. This was the state of our relationship: She was reduced to plying nonsensical facsimiles of the things we had said or done before, meaningless now, but tinged with futility and desperation. And I continued to accept them, smiling feebly all the while. Neither of us had anything to offer the other, but still we clung together. I thanked her and hugged her, and we kissed, but all the while I could not stop thinking of the object. The stuffed monster with octopus face, with incongruous cape and mask. This figure of consuming, incomprehensible despair, now a cutesy and not entirely convincing joke. I wondered that such a thing would enter my life, and what it meant.

We survived the semester. She decided to visit me in Boston over break, and I was not emotionally cognizant enough to refuse. We had a few weeks of sporadic contact, and then she arrived, a day or two after New Year's. Hoping to soften the blow should the improbable occur and I terminate our relationship, I made a deliberate effort to be as physically awkward and emotionally distant as possible during the visit. As I greeted her at the door of her aunt's house, she threw open the door and jumped into my arms. I returned her passionate embrace with one of proportionate discomfort. We spoke for several minutes on the porch, her perfect lips on the cusp of a kiss. I stuffed my hands in my pockets, and shuffled and tried to grin, pointedly refusing to acknowledge her.

We visited Faneuil Hall and the New England Aquarium; at the latter, the OCD casually noted how easy it would be for either of us to toss the other into the shark tank. We saw *Pan's Labyrinth* together in the theater, which is an excellent film but not one I would recommend as a date movie for young people considering suicide. Her hands regularly reached out for mine, but each time she found them diplomatically tucked into my pockets. We had planned to have dinner with my parents, but I tacitly discouraged this. During our early period of absurd infatuation, I had often imagined her meeting my family; it seemed natural that the people I cared most about in the world should be introduced as soon as possible. As her visit approached, however, the prospect had seemed less and less attractive. The idea of parading this mute, damaged person as a former future daughter-in-law seemed like it would be embarrassing and painful for all parties involved.

She told me that she'd gotten another tattoo, and I asked to see it. It was of a phoenix, a design she'd mentioned she'd been considering. I had suggested she consider the Dark Phoenix symbol used in *X-Men*, adopted by the heroine Jean Grey shortly before she goes insane, commits cosmic genocide by pushing a star to supernova, and kills herself; looking back, I clearly had not thought through the implications of this suggestion, although The Girl's unfamiliarity with the source material apparently stopped her from taking offense. The tattoo she had chosen, however, was a stately black-and-white affair, lovingly detailed, the fiery hawk stretching its wings across her pale and emaciated side. She cheerfully explained the symbolism to me. It was chosen because she had suffered in the past but she was better now, not like when she was better the last time but really for serious this time. Reborn from the ash into a state of perfect grace and stability. Celebrating her victory over self-mutilation by paying someone to dig needles into her skin. One might note that the phoenix mythology has other connotations beyond triumph over adversity; implicit in that moment of rebirth is the fact that soon enough that fucking bird is going down in flames all over again. If this occurred to me, I did not mention it.

Instead of eating with my family, we went for dinner with The Girl's aunt that night. The three of us were accompanied by a pale and lumpy out-of-state gentleman, apparently one of the aunt's former suitors from the Internet, who snickered and made suggestive remarks about the presentation of the rice. I went back to the aunt's house with The Girl afterward, where the two decided it would be appropriate to entertain me by cataloging their family's complete history of infidelity, spousal abuse, addiction, and mental illness. We sat there with the older woman, feigning casual interest despite our escalating anxiety, as she told us about horrible things.

Indeed, I had noticed that The Girl seemed increasingly uncomfortable throughout the evening. I confronted her after the conversation. I worried that she suspected my doubts about the relationship and prepared myself to reassure her. Actually, she told me, she was convinced she had AIDS.

This was her OCD at work; although she had recently tested negative, it had occurred to her that there still existed an infinitesimal possibility of infection, and this was enough for the disorder. She told me that shortly before we started dating, she had had unprotected sex with a man she'd met at a club. She said she was convinced by his assurances that he was clean, and that he totally got checked all the time, because he worried a lot about these things. I personally am stunned by the fact that she would question this gentleman's honor, because drunk guys who fuck nineteen-year-old girls without condoms are usually swell people; but as long as a sliver of doubt exists OCD is unfazed by rationality, and The Girl had become fascinated by the possibility that in this unfortunate incident she had somehow contracted HIV. In a moment of uncommon generosity she decided that I should share in her torturous, irrational anxiety.

In retrospect I am grateful; I do not know how long I would have endured, if not for such an absurdly unforgivable relationship faux pas. As far as these things go, telling your partner that you might have AIDS, after convincing him it was safe to have unprotected sex, is sort of a deal breaker. The fact that her worries were partially mitigated by her acknowledged mental illness did not really help her case. We decided together that night that things were not working, for now, and that she needed to seek professional help. We agreed to remain friends, and told each other that we might try to make our relationship work again, later, after she'd dealt with her problems. We broke up.

We decided to have breakfast together the next

morning as a way of cementing our continued affection for each other, and of building a foundation for what would certainly be a long and fruitful friendship. When I arrived, however, I found her wearing pajamas and stumbling around dreamily. It seemed that she had fainted that morning, shortly before my arrival. The Girl and I spoke on the porch one last time as the aunt looked on suspiciously. Absurdly, my pathological need for the approval of authority had kicked in here, and I confess that I was more worried that I had earned the scorn of this ridiculous woman whom I would never see again than for myself or the girl I had loved. So I hugged The Girl, and I gave her a kiss on the forehead, and I left her. I did not hear from her again until several days into the semester, when she phoned me one afternoon while I was working in the library to inform me that she (nonhypothetically, with absolute certainty) had chlamydia.

We didn't really talk much after that.

I was tested immediately, and repeatedly, so as to satisfy my own intolerance of uncertainty regarding infection. (I was demonstrated to be clear, mercifully, of both diseases.) The Girl transferred to another school at the end of that spring. We have not spoken since. The whole thing had been a farce, a cruel joke demonstrating the harm two people can inflict on themselves and each other with entirely sympathetic intentions. I sometimes imagine what might have happened if we had stayed together, if our guilt and need had somehow circumvented the inevitable; the psychological abominations our unnatural commingling would have produced. Perhaps that is something to be proud of, that I was in a relationship that might have produced a legitimate crime against God. Looking back there were two things I am genuinely thankful for. I think in the end we did love each other for a little while, as much as it was possible for our actual persons to evince themselves through our collective clusterfuck of symptoms. And I recognize that I might have gone undiagnosed for much, much longer had the stress of the relationship not exacerbated my disorder.

But it was difficult, then, to maintain perspective. I had stopped the medication, I was still trying to finish a semester at a comprehensive academic circle jerk, and I had survived a relationship that was effectively a one-man, twenty-four-hour suicide hotline. She was gone now, but it didn't matter.

This was how *obsessive-compulsive disorder* finally got me. She had been a door, and OCD walked through, and now I could not be rid of it. I could no longer escape or deny it. Nothing visibly changed, of course. I made jokes, worked, got drunk. I slept, breathed, ate and shat. You wouldn't have noticed anything. But I wasn't really there anymore. There was only obsession.

7

Countdown to Final Crisis

Life has pitfalls! Anti-Life is protection!
Life will make you doubt! Anti-Life will make you right!
—Jack Kirby, *The Forever People #3*

... and the anti-life equation = loneliness + alienation +
fear + despair + self-worth + mockery + condemna-
tion + misunderstanding × guilt × shame × failure × judgment n = y where y = hope and n = folly love = lies life = death
self = dark side
—Grant Morrison, *Seven Soldiers: Mister Miracle #3*

In his book *The Imp of the Mind,* psychologist Lee
Baer explores the intrusive thoughts that trouble many
OCD sufferers. The thoughts appear as recurring images that concern "whatever it is you consider to be
the most inappropriate or awful thing that you could
do" (9).

These thoughts are not exclusive to obsessive-compulsives. The human mind percolates at a tremendous rate and inevitably some of the random images it conjures will be unpleasant ones. Baer quotes an excerpt of Edgar Allan Poe's "The Imp of the Perverse," in which Poe considers the phenomenon:

"[There exists an] innate and primitive principle of human action, a paradoxical something, which we may call *Perverseness*. . . . Through its promptings we act, for the reason that we should *not*. In theory, no reason can be unreasonable: But, in fact, there is none more strong. . . . We stand upon the brink of a precipice. We peer into the abyss— we grow sick and dizzy. Our first impulse is to shrink from the danger. Unaccountably we remain. . . . It is merely the idea of what would be our sensations during the sweeping precipitancy of a fall from such a height. And this fall—this rushing annihilation . . . most ghastly and loathsome of all the ghastly and loathsome of images of death and suffering . . . for this very cause do we now the most vividly desire it. . . . We perpetuate them merely because we feel that we should *not*. Beyond or behind this, there is no intelligible principle." (3–4)

We all possess this quality of repugnance, this contrary drive *against*. When we say, "Right," part of us says, "Left"; when we say, "Good," some rebel aspect whispers, "Bad." The compulsion toward perversity is not something that we can ignore or suppress. The human mind is a complex, ugly, mysterious thing. Beyond the "I," beyond what we call our consciousness, dark and obstinate forces work. Alongside the bright Ariel of our intelligence there lurks a rude perverted Caliban; we call them conscious and subconscious, Freud's ego and id, the angel and the demon perched on your shoulders. We have named them a thousand times; we have a thousand times attempted to subject them to our will but never attained more than an uncomfortable truce. Because, contrary to the suggestions of society and religion, our minds are not and will never be entirely our own.

A healthy person can recognize this and can accept his perverse thoughts as an inconsequential by-product of the restless mind. But the obsessive-compulsive is astonished and disgusted, and the suggestion that he does not—cannot—control his own mind brings horror. The seduction of the disorder is subtle here. It suggests, not unreasonably, that the sufferer should if nothing else be able to control his own thinking. It pleads for certainty because the thoughts might secretly mean something terrible. So under the guidance of the disorder, the sufferer tells himself that his thoughts are meaningless. In his terror and his pride, he decides that with the sheer power of his will he will purge himself of these murky, irrational figments. He will subjugate his own mind, joylessly chain and shackle his imagination. He will name and catalog the unspeakable.

This task is impossible and insane. It is against life, against being. It will bring a person to violent, unrelenting war against his own consciousness and set him on a path that will inevitably lead to the crashing, violent implosion of the self. Implicit in any thought is the articulation of its opposite. The statement "I should not" cannot be expressed without "I should." The statement "I do not want to think about this" includes an implicit command: "Think about this." Because of this, any thought that we attempt to suppress will instead recur with greater frequency and strength. The very act of challenging the thought is what imbues it with such poisonous, irresistible strength. It is like quicksand, and the more violently you thrash and twist, the deeper you will sink. The old joke is to ask someone not to think about a white bear, and then watch them twitch in frustration as they find they cannot stop themselves from doing so. Try it. Do not think about a white bear. Do not think about murder or rape. Do not think about atrocity.

The compulsions are invisible and continuous. There

is no counting, no hand washing; the afflicted will instead lose years hiding behind a nervous smile, attempting to scrub clean his brain. The compulsions are a frenzy of panicked and desperate argument, endless pointless reassurance, the impotent application of reason and logic to sterilize dark places within the self. I would never do that I would never do that, again and again without end. Due to the absence of visible complications, this variant of the disorder is sometimes called "Pure-O," a name I like because it sounds like some kind of drug. It is not an unreasonable comparison. The more you use, the more you need.

The Imp of the Mind describes several cases of obsessive-compulsives who, in trying to eliminate their unwanted thoughts, are instead consumed by them. "[S]he thinks about how easy it would be to throw her defenseless Jessie against a wall and smash her skull" (xiii). "When he was an adolescent—although he was heterosexual—the worst thing [he] could think of was being gay, which could cause relentless teasing . . . whenever he saw an attractive boy in school or on the street or in the gym, he would find himself scanning his body to *try to feel certain* that he wasn't sexually aroused" (10). "[He] was now a liberal college student. . . . So now, if he saw an African-American walking toward him on the street, the urge would come to shout 'Nigger'" (11).

"Just a glance at the wagging tail was enough to start the bad thoughts—he felt compelled to stare at the dog's anus and his thoughts would start" (6).

None of these people wanted to fuck dogs, or to murder their children, or to doubt their sexuality or to scream racial slurs. Each of these was, in fact, the most unbelievable, abhorrent thing in the world to the person who imagined it, and this is exactly why it became tangled in obsession. The disorder finds purchase in the unthinkable. There is no unpleasant thought it will let you forget; it has no concept of decency or restraint. It will never avoid something because it is too disturbing, too utterly wrong, because it is in fact pathologically drawn to exactly these things. It is your boggart, your doppelgänger. It violates taboo naturally and thoughtlessly. It will reveal itself in school, in church, at weddings and funerals. It will inundate you, incessantly, remorselessly, with what are quite literally the most repulsive things you are capable of imagining.

So imagine the worst thing in the world.

Picture it. Construct it, carefully and deliberately, in your mind. Take all the time you need but be careful not to omit anything: the violence, the language, the fucking, the stabbing, the shit and blood and come and piss, endless perversion, utter desecration of anything good. Imagine it happening to you, to people you love. Imagine that you are committing it and that you cannot stop even though you desperately want to; imagine that you are committing it and you cannot stop because you love it. Look around, pick out the most vulnerable-looking person in the room. Imagine it happening to them.

Now try not to think about it. Try not to think about turning forty with a wife and child and realizing that you are gay, you have always been gay, and that you will lie to people you love for the rest of your life and that you will never really be happy again, ever. Try not to think about dropping to your knees and twisting open the dog's asshole, about clutching rough hair, about the animal yelping in pain as you thrust. Try not to think about burning a cross, about pissing on a crucifix. Try not to think about raping your mother with a broken bottle. Try not to think about crushing a child's face with a cinder block. Try not to think about molesting your sister, your nephew, your daughter; about huge fingers caressing dry and hairless genitals, about the look of absolute betrayal in uncomprehending eyes. Try not to think about the white bear. Forget everything, entirely. Now.

Imagine the worst thing in the world.

I returned to school after winter vacation an absolute train wreck, still staggering from the collapse of the relationship. Unfortunately this was around when my dorm room began to deteriorate. There are more agreeable places to lose one's mind than in a college dormitory. I did not expect pristine accommodations as a sophomore, but even by my lenient standards the construction and maintenance of the building my friends and I had chosen were frankly embarrassing. There were pipes in my room that carried warmth to the third floor of the building and produced so much excess heat I had to sleep in boxers by an open window in February; my roommate adopted a pair of putrid hermaphroditic African frogs, which could render a clean tank murky with shit within ten minutes; we had a rusty fire escape, which when removed by maintenance, left a hole in my wall large enough to stick your hand through. We realized that our unnecessary giant closet was directly underneath a bathroom because whenever the toilet overflowed we were greeted by a sudden cascade of fresh sewage. Swarthmore College offers specialized housing for students with unique medical needs, and I certainly would have requested to move had I not been preoccupied by the fact that I was sort of going insane.

I did not understand that from which I suffered. I recognized very quickly that that my mind was fixating uncontrollably on things that disturbed me, but I did not know why. I knew only that my thoughts were horrible and that they would not stop. I wondered, not unreasonably, if I was psychotic.

My grades began to slip. I applied for the fiction workshop and was once again rejected. Even though I was no longer taking medication I again began to indulge in marathon six-hour naps. I ate nothing but grilled cheese sandwiches and fries at the dining hall, yet somehow still lost ten pounds. I stayed out later and I drank more on weekends, never to excess necessarily: I never blacked out, no one noticed or tried to intervene. But there were nights when, quite deliberately, I would increase my intake of alcohol to quiet the voices in my head. Of course, when I awoke the next morning, I would be left with a terrible headache and the thoughts would still be there. Sometimes they would be stronger.

Later in the semester I would in my desperation seek out stronger addictives. In a fit of mad insight I downloaded from a German Web page an illegal copy of the Pokémon Trading Card Game adaptation for the Game Boy Color, a weird, recursive pop-cultural artifact, an incestuous mutation, a portable videogame adapted from a collectible trading card game adapted from another videogame. I recalled how my fascination with the game had distracted me from other, more destructive obsessions as a child, and I hoped that the creatures would do the same for me again. Terrified, I held up Psyduck and Mewtwo as protective totems against the madness. Surprisingly this worked for a little while, and whenever the delirium threatened I could quickly and supereffectively redirect my thoughts to the monsters. Unfortunately this tactic helped for only a few days before the disorder was able to overpower my defenses and again wrest control of my consciousness.

The obsession evidenced itself in the most absurd situations. I performed in a Tom Stoppard play and it was there as I waited backstage, dressed in full British military regalia, rehearsing lines about gazebos. I somehow allowed myself to be talked into representing my sketch comedy troupe at the annual Mr. Swarthmore competition and it was there as I marched down the runway to "Hot Blooded." I was in a friend's triple on a Friday night and we all bounced around and sang along to terrible music together, and it was there. I recognize a surreal quality as I look back at that evening, "Numa Numa" blaring from the speaker and my mind humming with atrocity.

One evening a friend from my comedy troupe, another sophomore I will call Jay, invited me to attend a workshop that he had arranged. The invitation surprised me. Out of all of my friends in the group, Jay was undoubtedly the filthiest, the one with the sickest and most utterly wrong sense of humor. His suggestions during scriptwriting sessions produced laughter and cringing in equal measure, and honestly I had never before felt entirely comfortable around him. I was intimidated by him, as I was by most strong personalities. And while I was pleasantly surprised by his invitation, the event itself baffled me. The bastard had invited me to attend a workshop on Buddhist meditation. This was not something I would have expected. Jay had developed a perfectly horrible Japanese Engrish voice as part of his arsenal of offensive racial accents, but aside from this he had never demonstrated any inclinations toward Eastern spirituality.

So one night we met in a classroom, and an old friend of Jay's family told us about meditation. It was disarmingly simple. You sit, and then you keep sitting. You concentrate on your breathing. If you find your mind running off in a thousand directions—and you *will* find your mind running off in a thousand directions, especially at first—you try to acknowledge the thought and bring your attention back to your breathing. You do not attempt to banish thought from your mind. You do not force yourself back into meditation. You let the thoughts be and then you go back to your breathing. There are countless books about meditation, and I've read a few of them, but I have told you in this paragraph everything I believe you need to know. It isn't the achievement of a meditative state, but rather the process of working toward it that is valuable. If you try it, you are perfect at it. Everyone can meditate exactly as well as everyone else.

I cannot say that the first time I attempted meditation was revelatory. I looked at people's shoes and I listened to the clock. I was a little bored, but I felt oddly
peaceful afterward. I thanked Jay and his friend for the
workshop, and when Jay started leading biweekly meditation meetings I attended whenever I could. But, predictably, I learned exactly the wrong thing from the
experience. Remembering the fleeting peace I'd obtained after the initial exercise, I came to view meditation as a medicine for my affliction, a psychological
Band-Aid that could cover my obsessions. Whenever
they became unbearable I would sit in a chair and stare
at a wall and feverishly wish them away. I was, of course,
doing it wrong, continuing the practice in exactly the
wrong way for exactly the wrong reasons. Instead of
learning to live with the miscellaneous contents of my
mind, I sat and breathed with the desperate hope of controlling them. Meditation became another tool the disorder used to take apart my sanity.

For the most part my friends were oblivious, and the
content of my obsessions was such that I did not, for
reasons that should be self-evident, feel comfortable
sharing them with others. Inasmuch as my compulsions
were visible they were fleeting and subtle; a wince or
a hard blink or a moment of inexplicable silence, the
only indicators of unceasing internal trauma. There were
moments when my friends noticed my unhappiness

and tried to bring me out of it, and I remain grateful. But human contact, especially with people I cared about, was a major trigger for my symptoms, and there were instances when even basic social interaction became agonizing. The intrusive thoughts became even more upsetting when they involved my friends and loved ones.

There were also moments of social antipathy among my acquaintances, small callous actions that given my circumstances became almost unbelievably cruel. I had a friend who delighted in calling me "emo." When I was being particularly melancholic, she would jokingly press her thumb and forefinger together as if holding something small and sharp, and then move her fingers over her arm in a teasing pantomime of self-mutilation. And I would smile and I'd do it, too, and we'd laugh together and the whole time I'd be thinking to myself: Don't knock it till you've tried it, babe. Of course, she had no way of knowing that I was suffering from mental illness, or that I had recently broken up with someone who regularly practiced self-mutilation and that I had sort of started to toy with it myself. She did not intend to cause offense. A harmless little joke about wrist slitting between friends, nothing more.

The only physical indicator that something had gone very, very wrong with my person was the resurgence of my chronic troubles with acid reflux. Throughout most of my childhood, I sometimes inexplicably vomited small amounts of stomach detritus into my mouth; as chronic conditions go I found this to be less bothersome than mental illness, although still gross. The reflux never really upset me when I was younger, as I soon came to understand it as a fact of existence. Indeed, I eventually became quite comfortable with the sudden rush of foodstuffs up my throat, hot currents of ice cream and ground-up hot dog, the penetrating burn of a mouthful of stomach acid or the shock of recognition as, amid a torrent of gastrointestinal sewage, I identified a bit of corn or a lone noodle intact. My father referred to this as "chewing my cud," and would scold me for doing so, but my family never saw this as a cause for concern. Late in middle school I finally broached the issue to a sympathetic pediatrician, who prescribed medication that seemed to end the problem.

The semester progressed, however, and soon I began to uncontrollably vomit little bits up into my mouth again. Disturbed, I mentioned it to a physician at the campus health center. He recommended that I get an ultrasound to ensure that I hadn't developed an ulcer, ignoring my objection that the problem had already been diagnosed. Better safe then sorry. I arranged an appointment for that Wednesday at the Springfield General Hospital, a couple of miles away from Swarthmore. I remember that morning well. Since I had not wanted to bother any of my friends by borrowing a car, I decided instead to take my bicycle. As it happened it was raining that morning: a heavy, smothering East Coast rain. I was already struggling with a minor cold and had needed to wake up early for the appointment. I also carried with me an assortment of heavy textbooks, each of which I was convinced I might need should I be forced to wait for my appointment, so as not to allow even a quarter of an hour of potentially productive academic time to be wasted. I rode along the side of the four-lane highway, cars appearing and then instantly vanishing from my narrow field of vision, raising thin trails of mist with their wheels. The ride was not long, but the obsessions were proving troublesome that morning, and it occurred to me how easy, how predictable it would be for my bicycle to skid against wet leaves or the crushed body of a squirrel, for my arms to jerk unexpectedly at the handlebars, for the bicycle to career out onto the hard, wet road. The possibility hung there, only barely acknowledged. Every kick against the pedals, I realized, every ragged breath held the possibility of a sudden violent death. Every moment I chose again whether to continue living or to die. The knowledge was exhilarating and terrifying, sickening, weirdly frustrating. For however much I desired it I could never quite persuade myself to turn the wheel.

I got to the hospital, and they took off my shirt and smeared grease all over my belly. They performed the scan and I was told that I appeared healthy. This answer did not surprise me.

Again and again I asked my therapist for an explanation of what I was experiencing, but she was content to reassure me. Despite my obvious unhappiness she neither recognized my symptoms nor, apparently, consulted peers or reference materials that could have allowed her to identify them. I made the initial diagnosis myself, over the Internet, because this is apparently the first place one should go for reliable information about psychological illness. I read the Wikipedia entry on OCD, and right there on the first fucking page of the article were the exact symptoms I was suffering from.

So that was that, I decided. With an explanation I had no need for further treatment, I could ignore the intrusive thoughts because I knew what they were. Things were quiet, for a while. Those thoughts aren't really me, I assured myself, a veneer of confidence masking growing suspicion, that's just the OCD talking. While I could tell myself that the bad thoughts were only OCD, I could never really be sure, and if I couldn't be sure, it would never be enough. I finished the semester, and my mother returned to take me home. I slept through most of the car ride. When I arrived at the house I found my family mostly unchanged, except for poor Bear, who had deteriorated badly since I'd last seen him. He was getting old for a Lab, almost ten years now, and early symptoms of dementia were setting in. He was clearly glad to see me—and I him—but occasionally he would be disturbed by some unknown trigger and bark until he was hoarse.

Having convinced myself that I was healthy enough to do so, I returned to work at the bookstore. It was here, set to interminable, monotonous labor, that my symptoms escalated beyond my ability to manage them. I carried textbooks back and forth, and I locked myself in the bathroom and imagined my fist against the mirror. I stood by the third-floor window and gazed out. I packaged returns. I helped customers and itched in strange places. Occasionally I would say, Enough. I would tell my mother as she drove me to work that I couldn't deal with it today. She'd argue a bit but eventually relent, and take me back home to play videogames. She seemed disappointed in me. I was certainly disappointed in myself.

I sought out a new therapist at home, a friend of my father's. Within an hour he confirmed my diagnosis and recommended that I seek specialized treatment. This official verification of my suspicions afforded me a few more days of mental quiet, as whenever the disorder manifested itself I could instantly dismiss it. My family had gone to Cape Cod that week, as we had every summer since my childhood. The place possessed a comforting familiarity. We went to shops that sold ugly cheap T-shirts, two for $5. We walked along the side of a marsh lined with tiny crab skeletons bleached out by the sun, which you could crush into dust with your hand. There I found an uneasy peace, for a little while. I read illegally downloaded comic books, played the Poké-mon game again on my computer, listened to music. I can distinctly remember the handful of albums I played again and again that week (Sonic Youth's *Daydream Nation*, The Replacements' *Let It Be, The Kinks Are the Village Green Preservation Society*), but while I usually form strong associations with music, when I listen to these albums today I experience only a hollow, frac-tured feeling; a lack of emotion, anti-nostalgia. I walked on the beach and scratched at my scalp at odd moments. And if I paused by the kitchen implements, if I glanced at a stranger and my fingers flexed and I turned away suddenly, no one noticed.

I lasted another two or three days at work once I was back at home. Understand: I never made a serious sui-cide attempt. Although I'd often thought about it, I never attempted deliberate self-mutilation. I always took the prescribed amount of drugs. But I would pause, some-times, by the knives or the railing, and dare myself to do it. I would try to convince myself, I would catalog my unhappiness and I would hope that eventually it would be enough and I would be brave enough or stu-pid enough to finally do it. It never came to actually planning anything. I did not attempt suicide, although I gestured at it.

Sometimes I would hold a razor at my wrist in the mornings, just hold it there for a moment and pray I could find the strength to press harder. Then my mom would call me, and I would put it back in the medicine cabinet and put on my shirt and tie and head off to work. I never meant to cut. But one morning I pulled it away, and there was a point of red on my arm, tiny and perfect. I gazed at it for a moment, and watched it shine and swell and then break, trickling down my forearm. I studied it, frightened, fully aware that I was not nearly frightened enough.

Understand that I never cut myself. It was barely a nick.

My mother entered the bathroom then. She saw my arm and she asked if I'd done that to myself. I told her I had. She called the bookstore to inform them that I would not be able to make it in today. I was sick. We went to the car, not speaking, and drove my sister to work.

Imagine the worst thing in the world.

She clutched my hand and did not let go. We did not speak. We were going to the hospital.

8

Living in Bethlehem

I could spend my whole life prying loose the secrets of the insane. These people are honest to a fault, and their naiveté has no peer but my own.
—André Breton, *The Surrealist Manifesto*

There was a song my father would sing for my sister and me when we were children, his version of Jerry Samuels's popular novelty song from the 1960s. *They're coming to take me away, ha ha, he he, ho ho. To the funny farm where life is beautiful all the time. Oh I'll be glad to see those nice young men in their clean white coats.* He gave a great performance, eyes bulging, his voice modulating and breaking, and my sister and I would crack up and beg him to sing it again. Then one day he refused, and when we asked him why, he told us that the song was disrespectful to the mentally ill. I never disagreed with him, but somehow I still found his response vaguely unsatisfying. I had a passing familiarity with the phrase *mentally ill,* but was unclear on its meaning. My only understanding of madness was derived entirely from old cartoons, from animated fish and fowl in straitjackets hooting and ricocheting off padded walls. That was what the song was making fun of, and who in their right mind could be offended by that? It wasn't about the mentally ill. It was about crazy people.

I remember leaving the emergency room that day. I was being taken to McLean Hospital in Belmont. The hospital was twenty minutes from my home, but in compliance with insurance regulations I was strapped to a wheeled stretcher and driven over in an ambulance. I remember my father crouching there next to me as we drove, genially conversing with the two attendants and sporadically squeezing my hand. Perhaps wisely, the three of them attempted to maintain at least the appearance of normal conversation. I occasionally tried to contribute to the discussion, but I could not sit up or move because of my restraints, and try as I might I could not prevent myself from thinking, *They're coming to take me away, ha ha. They're coming to take me away.*

The story picks up in the immediate aftermath of what may have been the lamest suicide attempt in recorded history. My mother took me into the emergency room and stayed with me until my father arrived to take her place. We were led to a small medical room where we waited for about eight hours until I was cleared for transfer to McLean. During that time my panic and desperation turned into quiet despair, which in turn became crushing boredom. I was driven to McLean Hospital late that night and was taken to a diagnostic unit, where I was told I would stay for two days or so while I completed some tests. At several points during my transfer from real hospital to mental hospital we had to pause so that I could perform for the pleasure of another group of psychiatric dignitaries. At each checkpoint I was asked to demonstrate that I was legitimately mentally ill and not letting myself be wheeled around in a straitjacket for the sheer, possibly fetishistic joy of it.

I was very uncomfortable discussing the specific content of my obsessions. I still am, to a certain extent; my symptoms represented my ugliest, most intimate horrors at a vulnerable and painfully recent stage of my life. Yet I quickly learned that only a small percentage of mental-health professionals were familiar with my form of the disorder. Despite its prevalence, intrusive-thoughts OCD lacks publicity, especially when compared to its beloved hand-washing cousin; within the spectrum of anxiety disorders there is apparently no image more compelling to the American public than that of some poor bastard scrubbing his hands until they bleed. This is what I found as I was pushed through the guts of McLean Hospital. The staff interpreted the perverse weirdness of my thoughts as either absolute psychosis or as callous detachment and sexual repression. Again and again I explained, as honestly and rationally as I could, the nature of my obsessions, and the nurse or receptionist would nod and smile distantly, wondering if I didn't have anything better to do than waste their time complaining about creepy fantasies.

When I was finally admitted it was well into the evening, and the institution was operating on a skeleton crew. Unfortunately, I had made the mistake of having my psychological breakdown immediately before a federal holiday. It was the weekend of July 4, and most of the McLean staff had been given a four-day vacation; it makes sense, I think, that those who attend to the needs of the deranged and the suicidal receive the same professional benefits as custodians and mailmen. As it happened, I spent almost a week on this diagnostic unit, among other patients whose conditions ranged from depression to acute schizophrenia, with only graveyard supervision. Most of this time I spent alone, nervously waiting for my doctors, who I sincerely hope were enjoying their barbecues and fireworks.

There were four wings on the diagnostic ward, with a large panopticon in the center. The place was like any other hospital, only more so. The décor was sterile, as one would expect, the walls painted sedating colors. Everything was monitored and rigid and deliberately, almost unnervingly harmless. The windows had cordless blinds and were reinforced with iron grating. There were no corners, no unlocked side rooms or closets, no places one could go if one desired privacy or quiet with only one exception: a single anteroom with a rug on the floor and a rocking chair, a token facsimile of a normal environment that we could enjoy under timed supervision. The door to my room had no lock.

It seems churlish to complain about the quality of food at a hospital, particularly a mental hospital, and to be fair McLean usually managed to exceed my very low expectations. The other patients and I were corralled into the dining room each morning, although I usually gathered up breakfast and ran back to my room as quickly as possible. It was always the same: plain oatmeal (I mixed in slices of banana), an apple, and a carton of skim milk. Dinner was worse, as I had asked the staff for vegetarian meals, which they were not accustomed to preparing. I was given green beans, black beans, a murky fluid that leaked out from the black beans, a plain Gardenburger patty without roll or condiments, a thin trickle of fluid from the Gardenburger. We were served with disposable plastic utensils, rather than stainless, so that we would be unable to injure ourselves.

Fortunately my family visited me regularly. They brought books and magazines and actual nutritive food. My father played chess with me to pass the time, and my mother spoke with me in my room. Even my younger sister, still working a volunteer summer job, managed regular visits. Although the hospital environment was deeply unsettling, she remained cheerful and sympathetic every time we spoke. If she was upset, I never heard about it. I know others whose struggles with mental health have been met with confusion or antipathy from their loved ones. My family remained steadfast through the duration of my treatment, and at no time ever was I more grateful for them.

I was initially placed in a double room with another young man, although I immediately and forcefully informed the staff that this would not be acceptable. Once I had been given a room of my own, I chose to spend most of my free time there. I listened a lot to my music player, although I had to go out to the panopticon to charge it, because they had confiscated my power cord so that I couldn't hang myself. I read and I sketched. I tried to write, and failed. I had blood drawn at least once a day. I played a game with myself, almost entirely out of spite, where I looked for ways to circumvent the hospital's precautions and kill myself: smother myself with a shower curtain, snap a plastic knife in half and stab it in my eye, shatter a lamp in the bathroom and slit my throat with the pieces. I took naps whenever possible, which was mercifully often because they kept me drugged to the gills. I was put on antipsychotics for several days, and one morning I awoke to find my hands shaking uncontrollably.

Eventually, after several long days of inactivity, I was allowed to meet with the professional doctors who would give me an official diagnosis. I took numerous tests, among them the Yale-Brown Obsessive Compulsive Scale (Y-BOCS), which I retook so many times over the coming months that I could almost recite it from memory. I had a meeting with the "team" they assembled for me: a psychiatrist, a therapist, several assistants, and a social worker. I was told my condition was severe enough to warrant consideration for treatment at the McLean OCD Institute, one of the leading facilities in the country for treatment of the disorder. However, my social worker was apparently unconvinced by my performance so far. She was a blond handsome woman with heavy makeup, and she listened skeptically to my explanation of my symptoms. She expressed concern as to my willingness to cooperate with the program, and observed pointedly that I had not attended any socialization groups since admission. This reflected negatively on me when the hospital made its decision of whether to offer me treatment at the Institute.

The socialization groups were regularly scheduled

activities developed to be accessible to patients at all levels of cognitive functionality. They included things like arts and crafts or exercise, and they struck me as perfunctory, almost insulting. More to the point: I was not even slightly interested in interacting with my fellow patients. Hopefully my narrative up to this point has demonstrated my pervasive social anxiety. And aside from that, I had already encountered many of the other patients in moments when I gathered food to eat in my room or when I darted out to use the bathroom. Many of them were afflicted with severe cognitive disorders and demonstrated symptoms that seemed far more debilitating than my own. I will be honest. They disturbed me. I like to believe that at another time, under less strained circumstances, I would have been able to treat my fellow sufferers with the compassion and respect that they deserved, but given my condition I had no interest whatsoever in casual social interaction.

I thus told the panel that I was here to be diagnosed and diagnosed only, and that I had no interest in participating in their activities. The social worker glared at me, barely restraining her contempt, and then my neurosis around authority kicked in. I winced as if struck and apologized profusely. My parents, who attended the meeting, smiled and agreed with the panel that I could be more social. If I was drawing sketches in my room anyway, my mother suggested, why not do it in the art room with other patients? After the meeting ended my parents took me aside. They told me that they completely understood my desire for isolation, but my mother, always canny, reminded me that my chances for receiving actual treatment would be significantly decreased if I did not cooperate.

Instead of retreating to my room with a bowl of lukewarm oatmeal and a mushy banana, as I usually did, I stuck around for the breakfast meeting the next morning. The other patients and I sat at small circular tables and were asked by the attending staff to state for the group our goals for the day. Gunter was first. Gunter was a bald, middle-aged man with a thick Eastern European accent. When asked, he stood up on the table and informed the rest of us with tremendous enthusiasm that he would today live up to his name, Gunter, Gunter, glorious name of God Gunter, and that he would be flying home tonight on the Frankenfurter. The rest of us stated our own goals, somewhat anticlimactically, and we settled back to breakfast. Someone turned on the television. The channel was set to VH1 and—I swear to God I wouldn't make something like this up—they were playing the video for Gnarls Barkley's "Crazy."

I laughed, and I laughed and laughed. Not because I

was particularly amused but because I could not imagine any other reasonable reaction. In any case, no one else seemed to find it funny.

Gunter was an inescapable presence on the ward. I rarely interacted directly with him, but at one point he convinced me to sign a petition stating that his cancer-stricken immigrant wife should run for president of the United States of America. "This place is a urine nation," he told me repeatedly, "it needs to become an alien nation." I signed and then, bless my poor obsessive-compulsive brain, I immediately started to panic, convinced my signature might somehow be legally binding. As time passed, I started to recognize the other patients on the ward as well. There was the obese woman with the piled-up hairdo and messy makeup who wheedled me, in a slurred voice, to set her up with my father. There was the kid a few years younger than me with whom I played chess and who had a disconcerting habit of tesseracting pieces around the board as fancy struck him. There was the small Russian woman who wandered the halls silently, always staring forward, like a ghost; a man who I think was her husband would visit and walk with her, holding her hand, neither of them speaking. There was the surly young poet with arms wrapped in bandages. There was the bulky Middle Eastern guy in his twenties, so thoroughly medicated he could only stomp around and drool. Once he emitted

an approving growl and stumbled toward a young female patient, hands positioned to grasp at her breasts. She
squealed in horror and he was immediately restrained.

There was the plump Jewish woman in her early fifties. She skip-walked like a child, teetering on too-small
high heels; she always wore a short purple dress, stretched
tight over her swollen stomach, so she looked like an
overripe plum. I encountered her once, eating a box of
Nilla Wafers in a chair near the panopticon. She asked
me to take the box from her, and when I declined she
snarled at me. "Take it," she hissed. I lifted the box from
her hands gingerly, and she explained surreptitiously
that she didn't want the patients to take the cookies
from her. I nodded and paused, unsure of how to proceed, then handed the box back to her. She nodded
back at me suspiciously but accepted it. Another time
when I encountered her in the same lounge, she was
moaning and sighing, hands smearing over her body
and head tilted back in ecstasy. *"Harold,"* she groaned. I
doubt that she would have noticed me—she seemed
preoccupied—but I was nonetheless careful not to at-
tract her attention.

I also met Lacey. Lacey was an elderly, compact woman
with a strong Boston accent. Lacey spoke to God. Not
in a metaphysical, spiritual way. Lacey and God had
regular conversations. She brought this up casually in
the halls one afternoon: "And I went into the house,"

she said, "because God told me to, and then the police came and took me to the hospital." As if her behavior was the most natural thing in the world, and as if the authorities had done something cruel and inexplicable by hospitalizing her. Lacey was fiercely evangelical and took every opportunity to profess her belief to others, to suggest teasingly that God could heal their mental disorders as he had hers. She would gather together some patients— the Russian woman and others, often directly outside my room—and they would sing dissonant hymns together and beg God to remove their afflictions. Lacey took a liking to me and sought me out each morning at breakfast to tell me that Jesus could save me from my illness. I politely declined. But it occurred to me, more than once, that Lacey might have been correct. My symptoms might have represented some kind of demonic presence; maybe I was being punished for leaving the Catholic Church. God might have abandoned me. The rational part of my mind tried to dismiss this as absurd, yet I could never state with absolute certainty that it was not true.

I was brought to the diagnostic unit largely as a formality, so that the hospital could confirm my disorder for its records and so I could later receive specialized treatment. The actual diagnosis might have been completed in less than a day. Yet there I was, in the immediate aftermath of a psychological breakdown, urged to engage in inane social performance with profoundly troubled people. I was vulnerable, my perverse and religious obsessions were triggered almost continuously, and had I been determined to hurt myself again, I am certain I could have done so without any difficulty. I can understand, in a regular medical hospital, the need for careful documentation and a regimented schedule for all patients. But admission to a mental institution implies that a patient may be fundamentally incapable of engaging in such prescribed behavior. The McLean diagnostic unit inflicted upon me arbitrary and unnecessary suffering, heedless of the fact that it was exacerbating the very disease I had been hospitalized for. I was kidnapped and blackmailed, and if I did not comply with my captors my best chance at sanity was forfeit. In a lifetime of dodgy psychological treatment, of countless moments of absurdity and incompetence, this was the weirdest and the most utterly senseless thing to happen to me. It was purgatory, an in-between place, a joke that seemed obvious and trite on every comprehensible level.

Apparently the alcoholics got their own diagnostic unit. Lucky bastards.

I did what was asked of me. I attended a gardening session and talked to a pretty young mother with postpartum depression; I went to fitness group and watched Lacey lob around a deflated basketball. I visited a seminar in the hospital's outpatient program a few hours after they changed my medication, and I drooled on my notebook and struggled to maintain consciousness. I met again with the treatment team and expressed utter contrition for my previous unenlightened attitude. I am ashamed to say that, in hopes of winning the approval of my caretakers, I told them I had actually learned a great deal from my fellow patients and that I was humbled and honored by the opportunity et cetera. I think I may have actually convinced myself I meant it. In any case, they let me go. The bulky social worker apparently decided I was redeemable. Now the real work could begin.

9

Midsummer

My escape from McLean was sudden, propulsive, like
leaping out through a window. Having been pushed,
filed, stamped, indexed, briefed, debriefed and num-
bered, I was finally discharged from the diagnostic unit
in mid-July. I was subsequently put into an outpatient
program at McLean, a sort of day camp for crazy people.
Although I was now ingesting .5 mg of Klonopin aka
clonazepam each morning and susceptible to brief
periods of unconsciousness while driving, I was free to
come and go from the hospital as I liked, and this did
much to improve my feelings toward the place. In my

classes I now associated with the damaged and the fractured but no longer the broken: burnouts and the survivors of halfhearted suicide attempts, silent wage laborers constantly verging on tears, lonely and despairing housewives. I saw a collage of tattoos across my peers' ruined skin. When I asked my transitional therapist about this, he told me that body modification was common among the mentally ill. Many of us have difficulty restraining sudden impulses or use variations of self-mutilation to cope with otherwise unbearable trauma.

Every day I attended several workshops, each covering useful disciplines for mad people, like mindfulness and impulse control. I remember almost nothing from these. Many of the ideas would come up again later in my treatment, during my second hospital stay and in sessions with private therapists, and would prove useful. I can attribute my obliviousness that summer to a number of factors: my fluctuating intake of medication, my terrible thoughts, and my lingering childlike resentment at being forced to take classes in the summertime when I should have been playing videogames instead. Perhaps I just wasn't ready yet.

During these interminable lectures I found reason to resume my old high school bathroom-break habits, although these were now defined not by self-loathing but by boredom and utter befuddlement at my circumstances. Here I would be made familiar with the infamous "urinary hesitancy" side effects of my medication, standing embarrassed before a urinal for long minutes before finally coaxing my bashful bladder to perform. By the sink, I noticed a perfunctory sign warning readers to wash their hands. It was scrawled with graffiti: NO YOU CAN'T GERMS ARE UNPREVENTABLE AND INESCAPABLE. It looked like the custodial staff had tried to bleach away the ink, but the marks were still scarred into the plastic.

Despite all of this, the outpatient program was valuable in that it provided me with schedule and structure in the weeks following my discharge. I needed this. It was a bloodsucking summer. These were strange and infuriating weeks, as I still hoped that I would be allowed to return to Swarthmore in August, but I had no opportunities to make real progress on my symptoms. Now unemployed, I kept myself busy with simple, useful tasks. I mowed the lawn and exercised. Together with my father I constructed a new case for my CD collection. I traveled to visit colleges with my sister and mother, and I finished the final Harry Potter novel; I cried, tersely and openly, at the death of an annoying supporting character, secretly grateful that I could still evince recognizable emotion through the fog of mental illness. Although seemingly tranquil, these days were infused with hushed tension.

As a consequence of my diagnosis, I started to pay

attention to popular depictions of the insane in American culture. Mental illness was no longer a curiosity tangential to my own experiences, but a subject of vested interest. I was one of *those* people now. If at some point in casual conversation, at a party over cocktails or Tupperware, someone asked if anyone had been in a mental asylum, I could no longer honestly answer "no." I had been strapped down, strange chemicals pumped through my veins, and I'd been locked in a hospital with iron bars on the windows. True, I had a fantastic anecdote to use in those icebreaking activities where they ask you to tell something unusual about yourself (I used to tell people about my jaw mutation), but the long-term implications of diagnosis were difficult to really wrap my brain around.

I found unrecognized, perhaps imaginary evidence of mental illness everywhere. No longer could a character in a film have a tortured conversation with his own reflection visually representing inner turmoil without evoking queasy impressions of schizophrenia. No longer could a manic cartoon character bounce and whoop without triggering thoughts of disease. Needless to say, depictions of real or fictional characters as "neat freaks" or "anal" or "really OCD" were especially touchy. The annoying sitcom roommate, forever scrubbing and sorting the belongings of the free-spirited protagonist, was no longer an irritant but a fellow victim.

Shortly after my discharge I read a review of the film *The Darjeeling Limited* that described director Wes Anderson, whose films often concern the oversaturated lives of stilted misfits, as being "like a filmmaker with obsessive-compulsive disorder." This perplexed and irritated me. Had Anderson's filmography, had *Rushmore* and *The Royal Tenenbaums* and *The Life Aquatic with Steve Zissou* consisted not of quippy dialogue and stylized acting but of a single looping shot of a bottle of hand sanitizer and sobbing, then perhaps this appraisal would have been fair. But the way things were, I am embarrassed to admit, the review made me just a little bit honest-to-God *offended*. As if someone had made an ignorant statement, unfounded in anything but useless stereotypes, that thoughtlessly trivialized not only my own experiences but also those of countless others like me.

A touch of electricity ran through me. Understand that as a privileged white Christian American male I have spent my life comfortably in the majority. At the same time, however, my bleeding-heart liberal education had gone to great efforts to explain the extent of the suffering inflicted by guys like me on everyone else. In a weird, masochistic way, I always sort of wished that I myself was in a minority, that with dignity and restraint I, too, could stand against the bigotry of a thousand privileged assholes. True, I was told that I could be an "ally," but that seemed to be a poor consolation compared to the real thing, the actual injustice I might, in another life, have been fortunate enough to endure. I am certain this was the reason the X-Men comics appealed to me so much as a teenager: this fantasy that I could be a part of a noble but beleaguered minority, fighting prejudice with telepathy and adamantium claws. And now I was. I was in a minority. I was overwhelmed by a sensation of terrible power. I could be oppressed! By God, I could be offended!

Reading that review I was also reminded of Woody Allen, who unlike Anderson actually *is* a filmmaker with obsessive-compulsive disorder. I feel about Woody Allen as a representative of OCD sufferers the same way I imagine some African Americans feel about, say, rapper and reality television personality Flavor Flav: initial amusement that quickly curdles into embarrassment. To further develop a troubled and probably ill-advised metaphor that engages volatile racial and social issues, I consider Allen's stuff to be sort of an anxiety-disorder equivalent of a minstrel show. It takes the complicated, vivid, painful experiences of living with a disorder and then abstracts them into easily digestible cartoons for the amusement of a clueless majority. As I watch his films, my response is the same as if he were dancing around in a straitjacket, drawing clockwise circles next to his temple with an extended index finger and repeating in falsetto, "Cuckoo, cuckoo." My jaw drops a little.

But my feelings about Woody Allen cannot compare to my reaction to the popular cable detective series *Monk*. My hatred is often tough to justify, because the program's creators are sincere in their advocacy for OCD sufferers, and the series features Tony Shalhoub who is something of a delight. *Monk* is the *Star Wars* of the obsessive-compulsploitation genre. It follows the misadventures of the eponymous mentally ill detective, misadventures I regret to inform you could accurately be described as wacky. That summer I stumbled onto *Monk* for the first time while channel surfing; my parents were made aware of my discovery by a sudden torrent of enraged cursing from the television room. Christ, I hate *Monk*. Despite its best intentions, the program gleefully depicts people like me as anal-retentive idiot savants. It's not just that OCD is equated with pathological neatness and only pathological neatness, which makes it awkward when I have to tell people that actually my type of OCD pesters me with graphic images of murder-fucking you. What makes it unbearable is that the detective-hero is somehow empowered by his disability, that his obsessions somehow enhance instead of annihilate his detective abilities. By counting and recounting, Monk discovers an important clue no one else could have found. OCD is a magical superpower, a clinical Shazam capable of transforming a whiny nebbish into the world's greatest detective. The program reached a nadir of psychiatric stupidity in an episode where the hero is pressured by his therapist to try medication. Bizarrely, Monk's meds completely and instantaneously obliterate his symptoms; unfortunately they also have the side effect of mutating him into an eighties cop-show douche bag. He snaps back into his regular, lovable, mentally ill self at the end of the episode, but only when a supporting character smacks him and tosses the pills into a Dumpster.

This episode encapsulates our culture's perspective on psychiatric treatment. Stop me if you've heard this one before: Madness is a curse, but also apparently a blessing, sort of like being Spider-Man. The mentally ill are granted unique, shamanic insight from their condition, and any treatment is cruel and counterproductive. Like every myth, this has some basis in reality. Its roots are entangled with the historical development of neuroscience, spanning centuries of cruelty and neglect: electroshock and chemical lobotomy, cutting bits out of the brain, Victorian Bedlam and Nazi mad science. And it is perpetuated, in popular culture and high art alike, in a thousand ways: by Oscar-winning performances lauded for their sensitivity and by cheap horror films set in grungy asylums, by Byronic heroes and by the ravings of comic book villains, and sometimes by celebrity-endorsed, sci fi–derived religious sects.

I find the teachings of the Church of Scientology

about mental health to be especially infuriating. Yes, I understand it is passé to make fun of Scientology; and yes, there are many obvious jokes, there are spaceships and ice lasers and cavemen and Lord Xenu—but most religious parables can seem ridiculous when removed from context. I cannot be too harsh on founder L. Ron Hubbard, either, because for all of his ranting the man did protest too much. He was clearly one of us. Hubbard, while furiously attacking patients and practitioners of psychology, was obviously bat-shit insane. I believe, however, that the contemporary propagation of this madman's beliefs by such a visible institution is reprehensible, and that their refusal to be held accountable under claims of religious freedom is asinine and cowardly. To watch a knife-faced movie star denigrate the mentally ill on morning television is absurd and hilarious, yes. But might someone perhaps also demonstrate some outrage? Is it unreasonable that I receive psychological treatment without having to suffer abuse from the alleged talents who brought us the renegade flyboy of *Top Gun* and *Hairspray*'s cross-dressing matriarch? You don't know the history of psychology, assholes. I do.

Again, not all of the church's criticisms of psychology are unfounded. I myself have been unfortunate enough to employ several psychs who, while not necessarily part of an intergalactic conspiracy, have at least caused me to suffer unnecessarily. But my therapists, while occasionally negligent or misinformed, have only tried to help. Are hyperactive brats misdiagnosed and hopped up on pills? Do corrupt multinationals advertise and overcharge for glorified nose candy? Have indefensible crimes been committed against the mentally ill in the name of science? Undeniably yes, to each of these. But there is a difference between the reasonable criticism of a flawed industry and simple narrow-mindedness. Survivors of mental illness are told that we have been duped, corrupted, stoned into submission. We are fools and victims. Or worse, we have been brought into the conspiracy: We ourselves are now working with the psychs in their campaign of narcotic oppression. We have conquered our brains only by ingesting Faustian pills and, chemically seduced, we serve dark new masters. Our submission to medication represents the abandonment of a noble and necessary burden in favor of personal gratification; taking medication is like Peter Parker tossing his web shooters and his red spandex into the trash and saying, "No more." We don't deserve to be healthy.

One of the reasons I resisted clinical diagnosis and treatment for so long was that I sincerely believed this. I was convinced that more rigorous medication and counseling would rid me of not only my pain but also my individuality. Over the course of my life I tried countless alternatives to cope with my illness. I tried to correct my unwanted thoughts with common sense and compassion, tried to convince myself that I could be sane if only I wished hard enough. I tried Western and Eastern religion, tried meditation, tried positive thinking. I tried self-esteem. I tried complaining to sympathetic counselors about my parents. I tried vitamins and exercise and thinking lovely thoughts, and in the end all of it left me curled up on the bathroom floor, a bloodied razor clutched in my fist.

I wish, now, that someone had challenged my prejudice against treatment, that I had allowed myself to internalize an alternate model of recovery. As I eventually learned, being sick does not make you a stronger or worthier person, and wanting to be healthy does not make you weak. Taking medicine will not change who you really are, and if it does, the medicine isn't being used properly. You don't need to hurt. You can get better.

But that summer I could only contort myself, miserable, trying to process the implications of my treatment even as I continued to wrestle with the bad thoughts. My mind had ignited. Everything radiated; everything burned. Everything I did, I did twitching, with manic drive and nervous laughter. I tried to write but I couldn't and I blamed the medication. I cursed, wept, paced my bedroom like a sick animal.

I did my best to hide my desperation from my family. While the stress of confronting the disorder overcame me only a few times, when it did it was spectacular. One evening my father took me out to dinner. We planned to visit a bookstore later. I mentioned offhandedly that I intended to buy a comic book; he replied, not entirely unreasonably, that as I was no longer employed it would be wise to decrease my spending. Perhaps his advice was a little unsympathetic, but my reaction was completely incommensurate. The argument escalated, and tempers flared. We ate dinner in silence, I was seething and on the verge of tears. When we left the restaurant and returned to the car my father asked me, gently, what was wrong.

My response was thorough and comprehensive. I hate you. I hate you and I hate Mom. I told my father that I hated him and my mother for what they did to me, for the accidental cruelty, for the staggering obliviousness; I hated them for failing to realize the blindingly obvious nature of my condition; I hated them for every moment of suffering and guilt I had experienced under their care for the past twenty years. It was their fault I was sick and I hated them more than I hated anything else in the world. My father listened silent through it all, quiet until finally I stuttered and slurred and broke down sobbing. He spoke then, not angrily. He put an arm around my shoulder and said things that I cannot remember, but he expressed only regret and sympathy for my circumstances. Fletch, I swear to God, if I could trade places with you I would in a heartbeat.

Because I don't want any misunderstandings I'm going to clarify the previous anecdote in painfully simple terms. Despite statements to the contrary made under duress, I do not actually hate my parents. I love my mom and dad. I cannot express how grateful I am for them.

The animals understood what was happening to me, the way animals always do. It would take months of counseling for my family to comprehend the extent of my sickness (a typical exchange: "How are you doing right now?" asks my father. "I'm imagining really terrible things happening to your left eyeball," I tell him. Cue laugh track), but the animals knew intuitively that something wasn't right. Bear was his dumb devoted self, slightly cowed by dementia at this point but still attendant. He made a habit, whenever I was trying to play videogames, of sauntering up to the couch and headbutting the controller from my hands so that I would scratch his back. Moonbeam, for his part, demonstrated an unprecedented level of concern for me. Moony was never a physically affectionate cat; he would debase himself to be held only unwillingly, his plump body limp and his eyes narrow with resentment. When he demonstrated warmth it was only on his own terms. But that summer, whenever I took a nap on the couch in the family room, I could pick him up and place him on my chest. Remarkably, he would flop over and fall asleep. As my prescriptions were adjusted I often found myself knocked out at entirely unreasonable hours, slipping into unconsciousness at the slightest opportunity. This wasn't entirely unpleasant. I have fond memories of drifting into druggy sleep, Moony curled up on my chest, Bear sprawled on a blanket on the floor next to us. They understood that something was wrong. In their own way, each tried to take care of me.

But I smoldered that summer. By the end of it I recognized a subtle, irreversible change in myself. It would not be the last over the duration of my treatment, nor the most profound, but it was shocking in its suddenness. I was now, beyond any possibility of denial or retraction of the diagnosis, mentally ill. Of course, I had always been mentally ill, and admittedly the word *depression* had been batted around in high school, but I had never allowed the label to stick. I was terrified of depression, of mental illness. These terms suggested a lasting burden, something that couldn't be shaken off, something that couldn't be meditated or medicated away. I was far more comfortable being bothered by my ephemeral, indefinable *something* than I was about having an officially recognized anxiety disorder. Now, for the first time, I confronted the fact that I possessed a permanent cognitive irregularity. It was part of me. This was exhilarating but also disquieting. To name something, I have been told, is to give it power. I was now and would forever be crazy.

So I submitted to the doctors and professionals I had

once been wary of. In high school I had taken medication, but unwillingly, and I quit as soon as I was allowed to. I could no longer refuse it. I was exhausted. I was still very much cognizant of that popular myth that psychiatry is the public face of a modern occult, eliminating individuality, reducing you to idiot narcotic bliss. As I surrendered to treatment, I was incredibly disappointed to learn that this was not true. Because, forgive me for saying so, I thought that it sounded *fantastic*.

Please, I told my new psychiatrist, give me some of these evil magic drugs that will turn me into an unfeeling plastic conformist robot, because I have experienced the alternative and if given the choice I will now take the blue pills over the red ones without hesitation or regret. Hit me with the hard stuff. Deny me my humanity, my individuality, anything that makes my life meaningful. Leave me a drooling idiot, leave me shitting the bed. Electrocute my brain. Saw open my skull and take out the naughty bits and then stitch up my scalp like Frankenstein. Make the bad thoughts go away. Do whatever you need to do to make the voices stop, but please do it as soon as you can.

I was denied. I learned, sadly, that no amount of chemical intervention would transform me into the corporate-controlled joy-robot I dreamed of becoming. I was told from the day I left the diagnostic ward that I could never actually eliminate my unwanted thoughts, that I would have the disorder until I die. I heard this countless times from a small army of OCD specialists, and yet each time I heard a clinical variation of the teacher's dialogue from old Charlie Brown cartoons, *wa-wa-wa-wa*. It was my new therapist, a warm and practical woman, who explained to me how I could make myself well: through self-administered psychological torture. At this point I was desperate to begin treatment, to banish the disorder forever—although, had I understood exactly the nature of the therapy, I doubt I would have been so enthusiastic.

10

Quarantine

"Philippe's been sticking his arm into the toilet for ten
minutes."
"That's his therapy for something that happened to him
when he was a pup."
"Oh." [Pause.] "How so?"
—Téodor and Mr. Bear, in Chris Onstad's Achewood,
October 23, 2001

He shut his eyes. It was more difficult than accepting an
intellectual discipline. It was a question of degrading
himself, mutilating himself. He had got to plunge into
the filthiest of filth. What was the most horrible, sickening thing of all?
—George Orwell, 1984

Working with the new psychologist, a specialist in OCD,
I finally began treatment specific to my disorder. OCD,
I was told, is a maladaptive response to fear: highly
specific, usually irrational, but nonetheless genuine fear.

Obsessive-compulsives are afflicted by a kind of hyper-awareness of the risks and uncertainties of everyday life. We are told, like everyone else, that we must practice proper hygiene or face viral infection, that we must say our prayers before bed to banish the possibility of hell. Ordinary people are generally content to submit to these protective actions only once or twice and then to accept that they have done all that they can. But a moderate response is never enough for the obsessive-compulsive. Everything is terrifying. Everything is death and corruption. To protect ourselves in a killing world we construct elaborate, ever-convoluting ritual behaviors: ceaseless hand washing to neutralize disease and prayer to stave off damnation, unending silent vigilance to ward off evil thoughts.

The hand washing, the counting, the prayer: This is compulsion, the ritual action necessitated by obsession and performed to neutralize the terror. Yet these rituals can never completely eliminate the uncertainty that drives the obsession: If you are unsatisfied with ten showers, is there really any greater security in twenty? Or two hundred? Thus the sufferer grows increasingly desperate. He begins to repeat his rituals, increasing their frequency and intensity, seduced by the possibility that soon he will rise to some unspecified plateau and then surmount the fear permanently. The rituals become overwhelming, unbearable, and entirely incommensurate to the original risk, yet even amid the frenzy of washing and crossing, the terror remains. Worse than plague, than damnation or atrocity.

As of this writing there is only one widely accepted therapeutic treatment for OCD. It is called Exposure Response Prevention (ERP). It requires patients to endure the fear without performing any of the reassuring compulsive behaviors. You are placed in a situation deliberately designed to exacerbate your anxiety. You are triggered. This is the exposure. Then, without benefit of ritual behavior, you endure it. Against near-pathological terror and constant temptation to revert to your embedded defensive behaviors, you endure it, utterly vulnerable, naked, and alone. You piss recklessly without cleaning, you sort without counting or count without sorting, you blaspheme without penance. This is the response prevention.

If the therapy is performed correctly, the sufferer eventually habituates to the anxiety. Finally recognizing the nonexistence of the feared consequences, despite the continued presence of the trigger, the patient's anxiety is reduced to the point that obsessive-compulsive behavior is no longer necessary or even appealing. The patient can subsequently endure future occasions of uncertainty without resorting to ritual behaviors and obsession.

But this process takes time, and it is far from painless.

Protective behaviors developed over years, over life-times, must be disassembled and then reconstructed. Well-worn cognitive pathways must be remapped. The therapy must be radical, must be traumatic, because otherwise the patient will never suffer the shock necessary for this fundamental restructuring. To heal, you need to break a little. And they will break you.

My therapist recommended that I make recordings of myself describing the content of my obsessions, so that I could listen to them repeatedly as a form of exposure. My mother subsequently took me to the electronics store to purchase a tape recorder, and although the attendant suggested I instead use the microphone function on my digital music player, we insisted on buying the recorder. My mother and I acknowledged, without directly admitting it, that we did not want any permanent digital copy of the recordings I would make; more importantly, we agreed that we did not want to create an association between a device I used frequently for pleasure and the therapy I would endure. The cost of the recorder was worth having the freedom to hide it away in a drawer, sometimes, and to try to forget that it existed.

So I took the thing home and made the tapes, and then I put on my father's oversized leather headphones and I listened. In each recording I described myself, in banality-of-evil monotone, performing some unthinkable act relevant to my symptoms. For about two weeks,

I sat alone in my room and stared at my ceiling, listening to these recordings on repeat. Each session lasted somewhere between a half hour and an hour, and while I was asked to perform two hours of therapy a day, I characteristically did much more. This was, predictably, a deeply unpleasant experience. Most of my time over those weeks was spent either in exposure therapy or dreading my next exposure therapy. When I slept, I had vivid and uncomfortable dreams.

As promised, I slowly grew accustomed to the content of the recordings. Yet when they began to bore me, they bored me for the wrong reasons. The tapes were so extreme in their content that I simply rejected them as implausible, absurd. I might as well have described myself, one eye patched, stroking my cat and threatening the planet with a doomsday device, so excessive were the scenarios I posited. The evil I suggested seemed unreal to me, and the disorder scoffed and worked to assault me with subtler fears, those quiet agonies that could not be evoked so artlessly. Thus I repeated each recording to the point of dull memorization, without a significant decline in my symptoms. The process was maddening and was quickly discontinued once I moved to the next stage of my treatment. I would eventually break apart the tapes, quite thoroughly, in hopes of catharsis and of destroying incriminating materials. If somehow reassembled, I imagine, they'd be enough to get me committed.

In late August, after several frustrating weeks spent performing independent ERP therapy, I was finally admitted to a day program at McLean Hospital's OCD Institute. The OCDI was much homier than the diagnostic ward had been, with a kitchen and a common room with couch and television. It was not entirely unlike—and was in retrospect significantly more habitable than—the dorms at Swarthmore, although the fact that a hostel for obsessive-compulsives was cleaner than a college dormitory really shouldn't surprise anyone. The furnishings in the public rooms were comfortable and worn from the activity of previous residents, but the bedrooms were oddly sterile. It was a halfway house, an in-between place. No one would ever decide they liked it so much they wanted to stay, and it was never possible to forget entirely the clinical nature of the facility. Evidence of the disorder was everywhere. It was like living in a haunted house; we shared it with a malevolent intelligence, a poltergeist, bodiless but ever arranging the environment to its liking. The halls were decorated with pouting supermodels and strings of seemingly random integers designed to trigger the symptoms of specific residents. To avoid indulging patients with contamination issues, paper towels were distributed by the staff on a strict as-needed basis. Soap came in little plastic medicine cups like the kind my mother used to measure out doses of cough syrup. Occasionally from a locked bathroom I would hear the sound of running water and then unintelligible screaming.

The original plan was that I would enroll in the Institute, overwrite years of painstakingly constructed maladaptive neurological programming in about ten days, maybe stand sobbing in the rain symbolically (weather permitting), and then return to Swarthmore utterly sane in time to purloin a "Welcome Class of 2011" mug from the admissions office.

I spent the better part of a week in the day program, driving to the asylum each morning and back home at night. Yet I had barely completed my orientation when I realized that treatment was not progressing according to my expectations. I was not getting better fast enough. My frustration led to another breakdown, there were a few moments of bratty suicidality, and it became apparent to my parents and therapists that I needed far more extensive treatment than could be administered in ten days. I was told that I could not return to Swarthmore that fall.

I took the news poorly. Through that torrid interminable swamp of a summer, it had been the promise of returning to my friends in the fall that held back the despair. I endured each obstacle and indignity confident that it would help me manage my suffering and that I would soon resume my education healthy and sane and happy. This all, of course, failed to take into account not only the severity of my symptoms but also my prior experiences at suddenly beloved Swarthmore. Looking back, I cannot imagine myself successfully returning that fall. It would have been insane to try.

My mother, ever practical, started to communicate these new plans to the college: arranging reimbursement for the semester's tuition, contacting the learning disabilities office and the student health center. Her extraordinary bureaucratic skills had thus far been ineffective in fighting the disorder, and I think we were both grateful that she had the opportunity to apply them productively. To help pass the time, and as a sort of karmic compensation for the setback, my mother and father also bought me a brand-new preowned and thoroughly obsolete PlayStation2. The idea was that, since we expected over the next few months I would have not inconsiderable amounts of leisure time, I could supplement my Nintendo Wii's meager software library with a bunch of old used games bought on the cheap. In a way, this represented the ultimate conclusion of the masochistic suffering-equals-prizes mechanism I had internalized as a child. If I sat through one of mother's meetings without crying, I got a plastic dinosaur; if I suffered from an anxiety disorder and tried to kill myself, I got a videogame system. Yet considering that I probably could have whined enough to swing an Xbox

360, or even a PS3, I like to think my acceptance of their charity was fairly reasonable.

My hospitalization that summer had fundamentally changed my relationship with my parents. Finally aware of the psychological shit I endured, they suddenly became permissive, acquiescent, utterly sympathetic. If a chore seemed unbearable, if I wanted a few dollars to buy a book or a cup of coffee, all I needed to do was play the O-card and it was done. Bluntly, had I been more of a manipulative bastard, I imagine the ordeal could have proven quite profitable indeed. Right now I could probably be living in the basement of their house, hairy and obese, permanently unemployed but with all of the free snacks and high-definition videogame systems I could ever desire. As repulsive as that seems, I begrudgingly admit it has a certain unhealthy appeal.

I began to contact my classmates through e-mail and, twitching on the hospital's lawn, I fibbed my way through phone conversations with concerned friends. Early on I had panicked, and recalling my miserable ultrasound at Springfield Hospital in Pennsylvania, I blurted out that I was taking a semester off for treatment of "stomach problems." I immediately wished I could retcon my alibi (a friend on the unit recommended "family issues"), but I was determined to keep my flimsy, blatantly fabricated story consistent. I would repeat the excuse to each concerned well-wisher I encountered, and if nothing else at least the total grossness of my story discouraged further questioning. Infuriatingly, I later realized I had overlooked an obvious, plausible excuse. I should have said that I was spending a semester abroad. Indeed, my situation was roughly analogous, except instead of getting drunk with Australians in Dublin I was living in a mental asylum and hanging out with my mom.

My family threw some essentials into the minivan (no need for the mini-fridge or the posters or for, God forbid, textbooks) and I started my second residency at McLean. I spent the first evening on the unit trying and failing to process the enormity of the adjustment. The staff had prepared dinner with the help of a handful of patients who had violent obsessions and who had been asked to cook with sharp implements as a form of exposure therapy. Regardless of whatever else I endured there, I have absolutely no complaints about the food at the OCDI; it was prepared fresh each night, and even though I was a vegetarian the staff accommodated my diet. It was terrific, despite being prepared (technically) by knife-wielding madmen. After dinner I was asked to help clean the mess. I took a drinking glass that had been discarded, squirted in some soap, and then proceeded to rinse it. The bubbly residue, however, was persistent. I rinsed the glass again, and then a third and a fourth time. A member of the staff had apparently been observing my efforts, and at this point he approached me and took the glass from my hand. "I think that's probably enough," he told me, not unkindly, and placed the still-soapy glass in the drying rack. "Oh, no," I said with a guilty laugh, "it's not like that. I don't have contamination issues, I have intrusive thoughts. I was just trying to . . ." But he smiled and insisted I rejoin the group in the dining hall. There was no point in arguing. I realized at that moment that I had no real response to his observation, that the disorder may have been far more pervasive than I had previously thought, and how different living at the OCDI would be from what I was accustomed to.

The staff at the OCDI was sympathetic and helpful, and a really unnecessary percentage of them were attractive young women. I am not sure whether to blame this on the malevolent gods of mental illness, taking another opportunity to vex our narrator, or on some inexplicable trend of hotness among psychology grad students interested in anxiety disorders. The only person there I didn't quite click with was my new social worker. She was a little bit older than my mother, with eye shadow and short spiky hair, and she was assigned to help facilitate communication between me and my family. She did her job well, I admit, and she taught my parents a great deal about how to negotiate with me when I was overcome by anxiety. But occasionally her suggestions were wildly inappropriate. Once, after I had worked through a period of suicidality, my family met with her to discuss how they could help me through such bouts of despair. Part of the problem, she suggested, was that the depression itself often prevented me from asking for help, and it might be useful for us to create a special term I could use to let them know when I was hurting badly. She suggested *crumping*.

Consider the implications of this for a moment. I am curled in the bathroom, pills strewn across the floor, rivulets of blood running from my slashed wrists. My father kicks the door off its hinges and my distraught parents rush in. Honey are you all right What's wrong Tell us. My face twisted with agony from the physical pain of my self-inflicted wounds and from seething psychological darkness, I manage a response. "Mom, Dad, please call the hospital. I'm crumping. I'm crumping really bad right now." Or perhaps I try to reassure them. "It's all right, Ma, I'm only crumping."

Or alternately, my family rushes into a packed auditorium where I, onstage in do-rag and sleeveless tee, pop and lock accompanied by phat old-skool beatz. "Fletch!" screams my mom, tears welling in her eyes. "We heard you were crumping!" "No, Mom," I say, and to the delight of the audience I incorporate an exaggerated shrug and eye roll into my routine. "Not crumping.

Krumping. You know, the school of street dance consisting of stylized jerky motions as popularized in the late sixties in Los Angeles?" And then everyone laughs, and my family runs onstage and gives me an enormous hug. And then I *am* suddenly overcome by suicidal despair, I *am* crumping, and I don't have any way to explain it to them. This is what I was concerned about. These are the situations I was trying to avoid.

And then my dad says that when I'm feeling depressed we should say that I'm "running out of gas" and we all agree yeah, "running out of gas" works fine.

In addition to group seminars and a rigid program of leisurely social activity with other mental patients, the OCDI required four hours of exposure response prevention therapy a day. Exposure here involved stupid, absurd, unhealthy things that no sane person would attempt. There was no chance that any of us could hide the nature of our symptoms. The constrained living conditions and the highly public nature of the exposures meant that each of us could easily observe exactly what sort of obsession had crippled the other patients. Simply through casual social interaction each of us learned about everyone else's deepest and most personal fear. It was not unusual for me to leave my room and find a middle-aged Hispanic man up to his elbows in biohazardous material. Those with primarily religious obsessions made blasphemous heavy-metal oaths to Satan. Those

with numerological obsessions contemplated evil arithmetic, foul equations with ruinous implications, comprehensible only to the sufferer.

My own exposures were less spectacular. I began by
discussing in uncomfortable detail with my therapist
the nature of my obsessions. My doctor at the OCDI
was a wife and mother, bright-eyed and cherubic. To
this chipper and maternal figure I explained the intrusive thoughts. Her response was disarmingly blunt. In
conversation she triggered my bad thoughts without
hesitation or mercy, making obscene comments with
jaw-dropping sexual frankness. This, she explained, was
what would help me get well. The tapes now proven ineffective, my therapist and I developed a new series of
public, social exposures, outside of the Institute. Obviously, because of the extreme content of my intrusive
thoughts, I could not really act out my obsessions for
any number of ethical and legal reasons. So instead
my exercises would place me in circumstances around
people that triggered my unwanted thoughts. I would
then tolerate these situations without attempting to
reduce my anxiety and negate the thoughts through
obsession. Essentially, I was being asked to humil-
iate myself publicly and to relish elaborate, horrifying
fantasies about innocent passersby, all for the benefit of
psychology.

My doctor accompanied me on my first public exposure. We perused explicit literature at a local bookstore; she took notes and offered suggestions as I blushed through an erotic encyclopedia. We observed which insinuations I found particularly upsetting and then made note of these so that I could later be clinically tormented by them. I continued by scanning the titles of the books on the shelves. Later I was invited to find particularly graphic hardbacks and magazines and take them to the store's café area, where I would spread them lovingly over the small coffeehouse tables, glossy sex pix visible for children and senior citizens alike. If anyone approached me, or even looked at me quizzically, I was instructed to smile politely and return to the literature.

Other times, when weather or transportation issues prevented me from leaving the unit, I was instructed to use the Internet to trigger my symptoms. I would call up YouTube, find a video with troubling imagery, then plug in my headphones and watch it on repeat for as long as an hour. As with the audio exposures, this quickly became maddeningly dull. This was my reverse *Clockwork Orange,* watching looping sequences of ultraviolence and the old in-and-out, unblinking and repulsed. My therapists were trying not to condition revulsion to sex and death but instead to desensitize me to them.

These absurd displays helped, initially. But the disorder, with cruel inevitability, found ways to tighten its grip. Its insinuations became subtler, more refined. My public exposures didn't require that I actually accept my intrusive thoughts, and they didn't necessarily mean that I was getting better. All they meant was that I was regularly making an ass of myself, and I was sort of getting used to it. This itself was not without therapeutic benefit with regards to self-confidence and social anxiety, but it did little to reduce my symptoms. In the face of unrelenting and clinically proven treatment, the disorder persevered. Weeks passed. The therapy continued, unrelenting, but without significant gains.

The only regular outside social contact I had was with my family. My college friends were all, of course, in Pennsylvania, and I was not particularly interested in explaining my current circumstances to any estranged high school acquaintances living in Boston. In many ways, the hospital's location was incredibly fortunate, because it was about a twenty-minute drive from my home, and my mother and father could drop by easily whenever they were needed. If I realized that I'd forgotten some minor necessity, my mother could be counted upon to materialize by the end of the day with the goods; my father and sister frequently visited to take me out for ice cream or a movie. On weekends I returned home for brief visits. Our activities together were never very exciting; often we'd share a meal and then I'd take a nap or play videogames. But I cannot overstate the relief I took in these short, unremarkable visits home.

The animals, too, played their part. My mother always made a big deal, whenever we talked on the phone, of telling me that Moonbeam had heard my voice and then forcing me to speak to the cat. I would sigh and protest but eventually talk to him, and he would apparently look at the phone and rub up against it, my mother all the while describing his behavior in a goofy falsetto. I suspect that both Moony and I were humoring her, at some cost to our dignity, but at least we were successful. I was also told that he always slept on my bed while I was gone. My mother took this as an indication that he missed me; I assume the fat bastard liked having all the space to himself. But he was clearly affected by my absence, and this is as much as one can expect from a cat. In addition, on odd afternoons my father would bring Bear to the hospital in the family minivan. Bear was an extraordinarily friendly dog, and while he mellowed somewhat in his old age I think that this actually helped to endear him to people. I'm not sure how the leaping and flailing and bastings of slobber he regularly inflicted on guests as a puppy would have gone over at the OCDI. In any case, I was always happy to see him, as were the other patients. Bear became incredibly popular, a minor hospital celebrity based on his few appearances. Very little was required of him: He rode over in the car with his head out the window, and he ran around sniffing and sneezing in the institution's shrubbery, but everyone flocked to him when he appeared. Much has been made of the therapeutic value of regular contact with animals. My experiences seem to support this.

When my family could not or was not allowed to be there with me I found other ways to cope. Although the OCDI specifically forbade drugs or alcohol, our counselors warned us that the stressful conditions of the OCDI would cause many of us to fall back into old bad habits. We were warned that now was probably not a good time to diet or to try to stop smoking. My early lapses were fairly innocuous. In high school, having failed to absorb adequate nutrition from standard school lunches, I often sated my hunger each afternoon at home with huge quantities of breakfast cereal. By the time I graduated, I had developed a Pavlovian psychological reaction to the mass consumption of processed carbohydrates, every night gorging myself into a happy stupor and unfailingly spoiling my appetite for supper. When I was subjected to the stressors at the OCDI, this hunger returned more voracious and arbitrary than ever before. I developed an unhealthy and annoying habit of waking each morning around two thirty or three and stumbling into the kitchen, able to return to sleep only once I had consumed a satisfactory quantity of breakfast treats. I am fairly certain that the night staff hated me, and I made every effort to apologize to them in my waking hours, but my nocturnal self did not care. I woke each morning like the wolfman, crumbs in my stubble and with no recollection of the previous night's gluttony.

As the treatment intensified I continued to lose control of my vices. Subsequently, I returned to gratuitous abuse of my personal narcotic of choice; once again I began to follow Pokémon online. Judge me not, reader. I was desperate and I took solace where I could find it. Someone saved my life tonight: Pikachu.

The other patients ranged from the apparently normal to those overwhelmed by the disorder. Yet they were, in defiance of popular stereotype, generally amiable and well-adjusted. No twitching neurotics here. A lifetime of unrelenting psychosis taught most of them to disguise their symptoms skillfully. My peers included poets, stockbrokers, police officers, activists, students, and scholars. Mothers and fathers and grandparents. Their compulsions manifested only in unobserved moments, in furtive gestures disguised by warm smiles.

Although many of us had antisocial tendencies, we were all drawn together by the desperation and the forced intimacy of our circumstances. We played board games and watched sitcoms, we traded stories and dumb inside jokes. We watched the Boston Red Sox together and we pissed off the night staff to no end, circled around the television together long past curfew, shouting and cursing at our team. I had never been a sports fan before, and had even come to despise the Sox in high school since they were so beloved among the popular kids. But encouraged by my fellow patients, I finally began to follow the team actively in the 2007 postseason. Their eventual triumph, the three-game comeback against the Indians and then sweeping the World Series against the Rockies, remains one of my fondest memories from the long, monotonous trudge of my hospitalization. Although they had already won a few seasons back, for me it felt like 2007 was the year they reversed the curse.

And in spite of myself I began to make friends. The New Jersey sorority girl. The endearingly venomous high school girl who was basically having none of this. The stocky gay Canadian guy, friendly and warm in spite of his contamination issues. The Hispanic kid with the model plane who would watch the same videos on YouTube until we all wanted to scream at him. The radical lesbian feminist, spiky-haired and bubbly and kind. The Midwestern Christian kid with whom I engaged in endless, unrepentantly geeky discussions about Nintendo. He brought his Wii and we played Super Smash Bros. Melee together, when his scrupulosity did not prevent him from doing so. Among all of the senseless human suffering I have seen perpetuated by OCD, this was among the most unreasonable: convincing someone that God did not want him to play Nintendo. The disorder was merciless.

A close friend of mine was a northeastern girl called

Sally, high school–aged although her education had been disrupted by sporadic outbreaks of her disorder. Each of us, patient and staff, was tremendously fond of her. She was sweet and sympathetic, she giggled with other young patients about rock stars she liked and she treated adults on the unit with respect and courtesy. She was unfailingly polite, optimistic, and sincere even while confronting a broad gauntlet of symptoms. These included contamination and grotesque sexual obsessions not unlike my own, but she also suffered from Tourette's syndrome. Tourette's is popularly recognized, and widely mocked, as causing uncontrollable swearing. This rare variation is referred to as coprolalia: literally "shit talking." On the one hand, I agree with the popular sentiment that swearing is usually awesome and hilarious, but I confess that I find the pure joy of language diminished when it is uttered without consent, croaked out with shame in gross, agonized tones. Regardless, Sally did not specifically suffer from the popularly recognized "funny" variant of Tourette's. She would occasionally wince, suddenly and uncontrollably; and then desperately try to suppress a whimper, as if she had placed her hand on a hot stove top but would absolutely not allow herself to scream.

She also had what as far as I know is a completely unique variation of OCD. Although I do not understand the exact nature of her symptoms, it seemed that Sally was obsessed with caring for others to the utmost limits of her ability. When you confided in her, she immediately assumed an expression of anguished compassion. "You know I'm sorry for you, right?" she'd ask, frantic. "You know I wish I could help you? Right?" And you couldn't tell her yes, couldn't tell her how grateful you were, because that was ritual reassurance and that would only make her condition worse. Such was the nature of the disorder that it could corrupt a young person's kindness and empathy. Her symptoms were irritating, just like all of our symptoms were irritating, but then hers became heartbreaking.

Occasionally, someone who simply could not stand the treatment would arrive. I had a roommate at one point who suffered from body dysmorphic disorder, who performed sit-ups almost continuously from his admittance to the moment of his discharge. His body was frankly terrifying, especially in comparison with my own, pudged as it was by long months of sloth and cereal and medication. I remember a middle-aged woman, perhaps in her fifties, with short dark hair and a perpetual frown. She did not speak, but she shook, visibly and constantly, for the duration of her stay. She looked like she was in agony. I never found out her name or the exact nature of her symptoms: only that they were severe enough to paralyze her utterly, to drive her from the one place that might have helped her.

I stayed even as other patients came and went, although I did not experience any notable progress. Through trial and error, my psychiatrist and I stumbled on an unconventional cocktail of Wellbutrin and Cymbalta, which reduced my anxiety without significant side effects. As I adapted to the more intense exposures, my therapist suggested subtler, deeper ones. Eventually, I reached a point where I would go to a local coffeehouse and then sit with a cup of chai, the mere presence of other human beings triggering my sickness. A civilian would walk by, and the disorder would drag my mind into all of the depraved and fascinating things that could be inflicted upon that person's body. And I would feel the overwhelming compulsion to resist, to escape, to scream in silence. To shout back that no, no I am a good boy I am a good boy now make the bad thoughts go away.

But I could not. This was the exposure: that I would open my mind to possibilities of psychosis and perversion, and that I would acknowledge them quietly, but allow them to be. I gazed into the abyss and, shuddering and biting my lip, I extended my middle finger and then plunged it deep into its stinking fundament.

Weeks passed, two, three, as I completed four hours of exposure therapy a day, and further troubles loomed. When my parents and therapists informed me that I couldn't go back to Swarthmore that fall, I decided in a moment of typical restraint and self-kindness that I was hell-bent on graduating as a member of my beloved class of 2009. To do so, I would enroll in night classes. At Harvard Extension School. While living in a mental hospital. In retrospect, it occurs to me that a psychological breakdown is probably about as good an excuse as any for postponing graduation, but at the time my perfectionist tendencies would not allow this.

When informed of this, my health-care insurance provider responded poorly and immediately informed my therapists that omg wtf. Their representative asked why, if I was well enough to resume my education, I needed to continue my treatment as a very, very expensive inpatient. As I am naturally inclined to believe the best in people, I like to pretend that they were worried about me, concerned that I would be spending unnecessary time in the hospital when I could have returned to school. In any case it was irrelevant. The only reason my therapist approved this frankly insane course of action was that she thought it would provide useful social exposure; that such experiences, carefully orchestrated by my treatment team, might help prepare me for my eventual full-time return to academia.

So, concurrently, I attended a second institution. Three nights a week, my parents would drive me from the hospital to Harvard, to interact with the sane elements of society. I took comparative religion and Shakespeare and economics. I was relieved to discover that, while the courses regularly plunged me into anxiety and obsession, just as often they would inspire crushing boredom. Indeed, while I actually enjoyed the former classes I decided the last was unworkable. The subject matter was too far removed from my own interests to be comprehensible; the teacher was a pompous buffoon. There was a very distinct moment when I realized that between the other courses and the regimented psychological torture I may have overcommitted myself.

I began to prepare myself to reaffirm my commitments, to steel myself for suffering and exhaustion as I had so many times in the past. And then I changed my mind. Enough. I unceremoniously dumped the economics class, and a weight—not overwhelming but still considerable—was lifted. I experienced disappointment but also tremendous relief. Having demanded from myself perfection and absolute effort, I stopped, and I said no. Perhaps, with enough sacrifice, I might have somehow completed that terrible class, but instead I chose to give my poor broken mind a little rest. Of course, the therapy continued, and the other two classes still allowed for lovely moments of surreality and literary weirdness. I'd leave a class on King Lear and then wait in Harvard Square for my father to drive me back to the asylum.

The treatment continued. Each day I returned to the café, ordered a large chai tea with syrup-flavored vanilla, and then retreated to an obscure corner to peruse pornographic literature. I did what I was told and I waited to get better.

What we eventually determined was that my progress was slow not because of the effectiveness of my treatment, but because of the attitude with which I was approaching it. It was, in retrospect, a simple application of my obsessive-compulsive attitudes to a new situation. I was suffering, and I had been told that if I did certain ridiculous things I could stop suffering, so I did these ridiculous things as frequently and as passionlessly as I could and waited for the sanity to return. I did not want to hurt. I did not want to become strange. If my symptoms could be reduced through flexibility and nonattachment, I would be rigidly flexible and observe the principles of nonattachment with military discipline. I was doing the therapy as if I were running flash cards for an exam or beating my skull against a brick wall. It became clear, eventually, that to get better I would need to reconcile myself not only with the content of my obsessions, but also with the persistence of obsession itself. It would take me a very long time to understand this.

I remember very distinctly sitting in the café one morning. If I remember correctly it was a Friday. I hunched at a table, leaning forward over a cup of tea, not reading Shakespeare or smut but staring, blankly, at the clock on the wall. It was a quarter to the hour. And

I decided, then, that perhaps I could survive the next fifteen minutes without being absolutely sure that I was not a pervert or murderer. I wasn't going anywhere. I probably would not, suddenly and irresistibly, do anything irredeemable during this time. Without trying to dispel the obsession, I might still be able to postpone my doomed attempt at resolving it for a quarter of an hour. Perhaps I could sit, and drink my tea, and allow myself to not know.

Consider the story of Isaac and Abraham—I'm stealing here, a bit, from old Søren Kierkegaard, from *Fear and Trembling*—but consider Abraham. God asked Abraham to do the most repugnant, blasphemous, damning thing he could imagine. He asked Abraham to kill, and not only to kill but to kill his child, to become a murderer and commit infanticide. He asked Abraham to do the worst thing in the world. And Abraham came to the mount and readied the knife, and for a moment he entered into a new cosmos in which he could be a child killer, and his god could be cruel and insane. In that moment of realization God said, "Enough." Only as Abraham faced the possibility of the unforgivable, of performing an act that was anathema to his person. Only as Abraham accepted that he could hate his god and destroy his son, only as he plunged the knife. Against the possibility of atrocity, against God's own word, Abraham trusted God. In that moment he was saved. Kierkegaard: "He drains in infinite resignation the deep sorrow of existence, he knows the bliss of infinity, he has felt the pain of renouncing everything, whatever is most precious in the world. . . ."

St. John of the Cross writes in one of his poems: "I came into the unknown / and stayed there unknowing / rising above all science." Science here, as scholar Willis Barnstone writes, refers not to any particular discipline but to man's constructs of "systematized knowledge." Unknowing. The original Spanish here reads *"no sabiendo,"* literally "not knowing," but I prefer the other translation. "Unknowing" something is the opposite of knowing it, and yet at the same time it is quite unlike forgetting. Forgetting is passive, it defies deliberate effort, and I think when we attempt to forget something intentionally instead we find our bad thoughts reinforced. Unknowing is not like this. It does not eliminate. It does not sterilize poisonous knowledge but instead processes it, subsumes it, incorporates it into a stronger and more flexible consciousness.

Consider the Zen Koan: First there is a mountain. Then there is no mountain. Then there is. We might ask, reasonably: what "is," exactly, in the last bit? But the presence or disappearance of the mountain here is made irrelevant. It is reduced to a mere quality of some incomprehensible and indescribable whole, big enough to encompass both negative and positive states. Through terror, through mourning, and then beyond into something else. Above all science.

Unknowing, resignation, is a submissive act. It is a release, a yielding. It is laying down a terrible burden, it is a process of liberation from the tyranny of perfect existence. Everything is taken away, even decency, even sanity; everything is lost except what truly matters. In a dead world of ice it is a resounding crack, and a sudden trickle of cold clear water. It is not painless. Like Evey in *V for Vendetta,* resigned to ignoble death behind the chemical sheds, like Daredevil in *Born Again.* Like Jean Grey becoming Phoenix in Grant Morrison's *X-Men:* There is warmth and then the bright moment of incineration. The breakdown of the rational. There's a cross, everything is a grid of hard intersecting lines, but then in the center there's a hot, soft light.

I sat alone in the café. There were moments of blinding terror, interspersed, and then a familiar sense of disappointment in myself, as if I had failed at some massive, incomprehensible task, had rejected a terrible responsibility that I had once long ago taken up. A tremendous weariness overcame me. Sad relief, a sort of acceptance. One quarter of an hour, and then another. The thoughts came. I sipped my tea. I suddenly felt very tired. When the bus arrived, I boarded it, and I returned to the asylum.

11

Songs from the Big Chair

"You know that apple Adam ate in the Garden of Eden,
referred to in the Bible? . . . You know what was in that
apple? Logic. Logic and intellectual stuff. That was all
that was in it. So—this is my point—what you have to
do is vomit it up if you want to see things as they really
are."

—J. D. Salinger, "Teddy"

. . . knowing a college education is a pile of shit is no
small lesson.

—Mark Vonnegut, *The Eden Express*

I left McLean Hospital in late October 2007. The day I
left I bade farewell to the doctors and to my peers, of-
fering each of the latter a careful handshake so as not to
exacerbate anyone's symptoms. I exchanged online contact information with a few. I told the Midwestern kid
to kick Ganon's ass for me in The Legend of Zelda.
I hugged my therapist. Throughout the process of

saying good-bye I remained, perplexingly, on the verge of tears. When I returned to the car, the meager possessions I had brought stuffed in a brown grocery bag beside me, I broke down entirely.

Even at the time, this baffled me. It would be absurd to suggest that I would miss the OCDI. Willingly or not, I had endured something not unlike psychological torture there. It wasn't the sort of place you drop by to reminisce, and the few times that circumstances have required me to return to McLean since then I have experienced minor panic attacks. But something profound had occurred during my time at the Institute, and because of this my departure was an emotionally seismic event. I find it interesting to compare my emotions at my arrival with those I experienced upon leaving. When I first came to the OCDI, when I was told my treatment would take not days but months, I broke down; I resorted to suicidality almost out of habit, lacking any way to cope with disappointment other than with fantasies of self-annihilation. Yet when I left the place I cried. This reaction did not make sense at the time, and it certainly lacked the urgency of my previous impulse toward self-destruction, but somehow it felt more honest. Even now, I have difficulty explaining the emotions I experienced as I left that place. I do not know what made me cry. I believe it was gratitude. Or possibly Stockholm syndrome.

Because of the divisions between academic semesters I would not be allowed to return to college until January. I was now twice removed from reality, exiled from the ivory womb that had incubated my madness. Directionless, I played videogames and baked cookies with my mother; I finished my night classes. I am not the sort of person who takes pleasure in boasting of academic achievements, but I am pleased to say that I earned a B+ and a straight-up A in the two courses I managed to finish. Of course, the classes were not as challenging as those at Swarthmore, and I took only two instead of the usual four, but I am certain that my academic performance was at least partially compromised by the fact that I was living in a motherfucking mental institution. Taking all of this into account, I think I did pretty well.

I also took a job at a local record store in hopes of restoring some of the savings I'd spent, as well as preserving some scrap of my remaining indie cred. (Unfortunately while hospitalized I neglected my duty to listen to and scoff at new, popular music. My little sister, bless her, told me that living in a mental asylum was "pretty indie rock." I acknowledge that several times at McLean I caught myself wondering if the hospital sold T-shirts that I might purchase and wear faux-ironically, perhaps underneath a fitted blazer.) The store was called Newbury Comics, a small Boston-area chain shop that was no longer exclusively on Newbury Street and no longer exclusively sold comic books: In the prehistoric past of Boston chain retail, it expanded to sell first music and later any and all forms of pop culture detritus. I respect Newbury Comics for its willingness to sell anything and everything, as long as it is popular. The company is quirky and eclectic in the most mercenary way possible. The place is a pop Babylon, the warehouse of America's id. Vinyl records and compact discs, comic books, Red Sox memorabilia, little overpriced Japanese action figures, children's trading cards in a glass case next to hardcore pornography, budget-priced cult DVDs without any discernible cult. Little plastic polar bears that pooped out chocolate jellybeans. We sold novelty women's underwear made from candy, and a customer once called to ask if we had the same for men. I told him we didn't and he asked when we might get it in. "I'm sorry, sir, but that product does not actually exist, because if it did it would herald the apocalypse."

I had tried and failed every summer since high school to get a job at Newbury Comics (or "The Noob," as I called it, with my mother and never under any circumstances in front of anyone else), and I was generally quite happy to be working there. If nothing else, the employee discount I got on comic books and used CDs would probably have been payment enough. The work was not dramatically different from what I used to do at the bookstore, but the place's unique atmosphere and my greater understanding of my disorder allowed me to manage my remaining symptoms.

Although I had been released from McLean, I was still experiencing symptoms regularly. I was better without necessarily being well. Sometimes while shelving inventory I would recognize an unpleasant thought of the sort that, before, would have sent me spiraling into obsession. My response was immediate. I attacked it. Remember that the best treatment for purely obsessional OCD is to resign oneself to the possibility that the feared situation might actually occur. Thus at the earliest suggestion of an uncomfortable figment, I would begin an unrelenting litany of awful imagery, running through a carefully constructed cycle of oaths and blasphemies. I would chant in my mind all of the terrible things that I might have wanted to do, crossing my fingers all the while and waiting for the disease to relent. I tried to kill the OCD. But frustratingly, while I was doing everything right, I found that these strategies suppressed the disorder only rarely and just as often perpetuated it. Try as we might, my therapist and I could not determine why, and it would take long months of treatment before I worked out exactly what I was still obsessed with.

But the disorder was really more of an irritant now. It would occasionally discourage me through its sheer persistence, but even when this happened I knew how to endure it. The symptoms were confusing, annoying,

often profoundly disturbing, but because I now understood where they came from and how to work against
them, they no longer had absolute power over me. While
they still occurred, sometimes for days at a time, I was
able to manage them.

The job was only part-time, and somehow I survived
those long, insufferable weeks of delicious food and abun-
dant leisure. But I constantly reminded myself that
soon I would return to the academic dungeon, and
January became like an evil Christmas to me; I had a
small plastic case I used to sort out my daily phalanx of
pills, and each day I opened it like some unholy advent
calendar, swallowing the bitter narcotic chocolate and
counting the days until judgment, my trial without
jury or sanity clause, was delivered.

In late January my father drove me back to Philadelphia. When we got there my friends welcomed me enthusiastically, but otherwise my return was uneventful
and generally uncommented on. I parroted my grotesque alibi and found it unquestioned. I quietly slipped
back into my established social circles. I was cast in a play
and began new courses. My education continued. Yet
my extensive study at a more selective, arguably more
rigorous institution (Fletcher's Skull Community College) had irreversibly altered my perspective. Everything
seemed smaller now. The laborious academic discourse I
had once accepted without question now seemed pedan-

tic and trivial. Classmates would complain about double-credit laboratory seminar take-home theses, and I would stare, mute and blinking, uncomprehending of a language I had once spoken fluently.

Part of this was that I was no longer willing to engage in the ecstatic ritual flagellation of my fellow monastics. My symptoms, after all, were exacerbated by stress, so I was told to reduce my academic commitments and, when necessary, to slack unapologetically. I met with the disabilities coordinator to discuss how my teachers could compensate for my madness, and I was told that I could parlay the O-card into late homework passes whenever I liked. This was helpful, but it did not always compensate for the idiosyncrasies of the disorder. When asked to post to a class discussion board, I would wince and ruminate; an hour spent studying instead of sleeping was an hour in the company of screaming ghosts. I imagine that Swarthmore's faculty does not bother with the literary endeavors of its alumni, but a plea, if any of you are reading: restraint, compassion. Every time I was pushed beyond my ability to cope I fucking suffered a little. I suspect that I was not the only one.

I recognized the boundaries of a moral dilemma here, the sort of thing that would have given me fits before my treatment. Each time I was tempted to ask my professors for the extension they were legally obligated to give me I wondered: Am I really doing this so I can take time to deal with the OCD, or am I just being lazy, taking advantage of the school, and making it harder for the students with real learning disabilities who actually need special considerations? Eventually I resolved that I did not give a fuck or even a small fraction of a fuck or even a small fraction thereof. Swarthmore was absurd. Swarthmore sucked. It was playing the school's incomprehensible game that initially dragged me down into madness. I would take every concession they would give me. If that was cheating, well, the game had been rigged from the start, and I was done trying to win on their terms. All I wanted now was to graduate. If I could accomplish this with a GPA, not any GPA in particular but literally any number they were willing to concede, I would be happy.

Also, that spring, after three years of trying, I finally got into the fiction workshop. I attribute this partially to the fact that the professor teaching the course was a science-fiction writer, sympathetic to the sort of work I produced, and partially to my shameless pimping of my mental illness in my cover letter. "Should I be allowed into the workshop, I imagine much of my work will deal with being *mentally ill,* because I am *mentally ill,* and am interested in addressing themes of *mental illness.* Did I mention I went to McLean Hospital? *The* McLean Hospital? Because I'm *mentally ill?*" There is a respectable canon of mad writers offing themselves to general critical acclaim: Woolf and Hemingway all the way through David Foster Wallace. I was determined to bully my way into their ranks, dignity and actual literary merit be damned.

Of course my reintegration into Swarthmore required more than compromised academic pursuits. When I first returned I made some awkward attempts to return to the Swarthmore party scene. These expeditions met with failure, and I would wisely abandon them after only eleven months or so. My brain chemistry was at this point well and thoroughly fucked by Cymbalta and Wellbutrin, and my alcohol tolerance was adjusted accordingly. Even a few beers could induce a swooning drunk at first undetectable until it arrived in a sudden vertiginous rush, and which could continue well into the following afternoon. I didn't have hangovers, which would have been great, but instead of getting hangovers I just stayed drunk.

Similarly, while the OCDI had taught me many things about myself and my disorder, three months of hospitalization and *Clockwork Orange*–style exposure to disturbing sexual imagery did little to increase my comfort around women. Indeed, I had been celibate for more than a year now, and returning to school I was possessed by manic desperation. I assured my parents, and my therapists, and myself, that I would be careful and not rush into a relationship until I was ready. When I got to school it took about five days before I found a new girlfriend. Our relationship was a textbook case of the doomed college romance: drunken commingling followed by sporadic contact and stilted conversation, followed by the inevitable acknowledgment that we had absolutely nothing in common. It lasted a little less than two weeks. Looking back, I think it was something I needed to get through. I'm grateful no one got hurt.

These misadventures continued steadily downhill. It was not that the concept of horrible meaningless sex had lost its ugly appeal, but it became increasingly clear that horrible meaningless sex was not to be had at Swarthmore. In classic obsessive-compulsive fashion, that didn't prevent me from trying. I continued to employ the familiar, idiotic seduction strategies I had been failing with since my freshman year. I stood in dark corners at parties, attempted tipsy kisses at highly inappropriate moments against resentful targets. This had all sort of worked before, but I was much older now, and what had been harmless and inoffensive as an easily beaten-up freshman became faintly embarrassing as an upperclassman. My classmates had experienced an additional semester of ordinary college social life, or had studied abroad with sultry European bastards, and through these experiences had either grown more subtle in their hedonism or gotten over the need for casual encounters entirely. Most of the friends I had once fussed over as wonderful drunks now had steady girlfriends and inflexible study schedules. This is not to say that I was entirely unsuccessful, that I did not occasionally find women who were interested in me, yet against each modest success there would be another morning when I would wake up alone and intoxicated, and then suddenly become hot with shame as I remembered the idiot failure of the previous night.

It took me much longer than it should have, but eventually I realized that my biochemistry and fractured psychology were no longer capable of supporting ordinary collegiate adventures. I wish that I could confine this stupidity to the prediagnosis chapters of the book, that I could dismiss it as a by-product of my broken mind. But that would be dishonest. One of the things that has been impressed upon me through my treatment is the continuous nature of therapy; while I made progress in one area, there remained work to be done in others. Sanity is not equivalent to maturity. I had finally succeeded in becoming a functioning adolescent just in time to be an adult.

By strange coincidence, Swarthmore was actually quite close to the Anxiety & Agoraphobia Treatment Center just outside Philadelphia. My therapist at the OCDI had been delighted to realize this, although I was warned by the staff that the center's director, Jon Grayson, was considered something of a rock star. The fact that there exists anything resembling "rock star" status in the realm of OCD treatment boggles the mind. But I met the doctor for a consultation and he seemed nice enough, although I am predisposed to think highly of anyone who keeps reading *X-Men* even after receiving his Ph.D.

Grayson agreed to take me as a patient, and he set me up with a new OCD specialist. His name was Sal, and although I tried to call him doctor he insisted that I refer to him only as Sal. I replied that I preferred to reinforce the therapist–patient power structure by using his surname, and that to do otherwise would make me feel highly uncomfortable. And then I remembered, with some prodding from my new therapist, that most of my progress had occurred when and only when I was highly uncomfortable. He had me there, the bastard. This was sort of a trump card for Sal during the course of our work together. Whenever I hesitated, whenever the treatment made me feel queasy, all he needed to do was to remind me of my time at the OCDI and the good it had done. Having endured everything else, I was now incapable of choosing the path of least resistance in treatment. I'd been there before, I knew that road, and I knew exactly where it ended. It wasn't where I wanted to be.

The gentle therapeutic prods continued because I was still sometimes bothered by intrusive thoughts. I had long since learned to manage their suggestions, to steel myself against the unthinkable scenarios they implied. Occasionally, Sal would lead me in a guided exposure exercise, and he would listen as I went on for upward of fifteen minutes in an id-driven, stream-of-conscious litany of atrocities. But by now the imagery seemed almost mundane. When the thoughts occurred I was panicked, not necessarily by their content, but rather by the maddening persistence of the obsession. OCD methodically exploits its host's deepest and most personal fears. That spring, the thing that frightened me more than anything else was my own obsessive-compulsive disorder. Each new intrusion might have been a portent of the disorder's reemergence, a new reprisal of the misery of the past twenty years. I was instructed, as I had been at the OCDI, to respond to the thoughts with equal perversity; thus I developed a protective chant, a rosary of cursing and wickedness recited to banish the disorder from my mind. Compulsion masquerading as exposure. Sal, to his credit, eventually recognized that the sexual and violent content of my thoughts was no longer the actual object of my obsessions. He informed me that somehow, gloriously and maddeningly, I had begun to obsess about obsessing.

This is not an entirely unknown phenomenon in the study of anxiety disorders, but the implications were faintly baffling. In an insane crossover of academia with mental illness, I had developed postmodern OCD, and as I adjusted to each new layer of neurosis, the disorder continued to outpace me. Even as I adapted, it continued to perplex my efforts; when I realized I was obsessing about obsessing and tried to stop, it asked if I was now obsessing about obsessing about obsessing; obsession and obsession and obsession, layers of thought enveloping one another like an inverse onion. Was I obsessing now? What about now? These questions did not cease and could not be answered. Escalation. Like the Red Queen's race in Lewis Carroll's *Through the Looking-Glass*. It took all of my running of all my mind, only to keep in the same place.

Sal and I struggled with this for months. Every Friday that spring I traveled over to his office by car share or public bus, and we spent a long hour trying to disentangle my thinking. We tried endless, circular exposures, we confronted the thoughts that reinforced the obsession that drew their momentum from being thought. Each time I attacked it with another form of preventative exposure, the OCD tightened its grip.

There was no sudden moment of revelation in this stage of my treatment, no epiphany. I experienced countless relapses and committed indefensible blunders. The answer, of course, was stupidly obvious from the beginning, and the only obstacle was my steadfast refusal to see it. I was demanding perfect treatment, perfect health.

As I had in the hospital, I was still trying to apply obsessive-compulsive logic to my struggle against OCD. It fed upon the sadness and anger directed against it: lean morsels, to be sure, compared to the feast of neurosis it had gorged itself on, but enough to ensure a meager existence. Every time I demanded that it vanish, it stole back from me a tiny fragment of my mind.

What I slowly, agonizingly accepted was that I would never be fully healthy. Paradoxically, I overcame the sickness in doing so. This is what I learned: I am not healed and I never can be. I cannot eliminate my unwanted thoughts, and although I am learning to manage them, I will experience sporadic outbreaks of symptoms for the rest of my life. I will never extract myself from the sterilizing, controlling, self-annihilating tendencies that I have struggled with since childhood. I will have my disorder until I die. But I am healing, I will continue healing. This is enough. It has to be.

It should have been enough, anyway, but my battles with mental illness no longer took place entirely inside my mind. There were odd moments of discontinuity following my return to Swarthmore, resonances that others missed, inside jokes that would confound anyone sane. There were times when I felt an overwhelming urge to speak up, to scream until hoarse and raw-throated. When I first returned to school, my mother and I met with my academic adviser and told him what had happened. He nodded blankly and told me that he was relieved that, after all, it was only OCD. His obliviousness was the norm rather than the exception. At parties, I encountered weekend bingers who would tell me, joint or screwdriver in hand, that they did not believe psychiatric medication was a valid form of medical treatment. I had conversations with strained acquaintances over dinner, each sloppily masticating as they regaled me with tales of academic conquests, complaining blissfully about their achievements; and then chuckling, claiming that the intellectual rigor of their activities made them totally oh-cee-dee. I was subjected to periodic published diatribes, composed by undergraduate fuckwits manic on Nietzsche and caffeine and sleep deprivation, that claimed that mental illness did not exist; that all I must do is believe, and the Power of my Will shall elevate me to glorious rationality. I was told that medicine is unnecessary because unnecessary suffering is the medicine, and I was told that it is my fault that I was tortured because I did not want enough to be healthy.

In these moments it was difficult to find an ear wired up to a sympathetic brain. On a campus cross sectioned by clashing minority identities, driven by numb sensitivity and mob correctness, I quickly discovered that those afflicted with mental illness were the first to be silenced. We were alike but alone. We had no history of oppression or triumph to draw strength from, no artists or advocates to champion our cause; no academic department dedicated to cataloging our achievements, although our behavior was carefully and clinically examined, like that of dogs or rats.

Alone, still hiding my sickness, I could do only so much about this sort of thing, but as a senior I started to volunteer with the school's peer-counseling group. I met some remarkable people. While I wish to respect the privacy of my friends, it should not surprise the reader that some of them had experience with mental illness, either personally or within their family, and it was a tremendous relief to find a space where these issues could be discussed openly. That year we ran a handful of events promoting the awareness of mental illness. We didn't do anything really elaborate. We had a tremendously stilted open discussion of mental-health issues on campus, which in retrospect we should have been better prepared for, although in fairness I think only one person broke down sobbing. We plastered the campus with pictures of adorable puppies. One night we gathered under cover of darkness, to scrawl across sidewalks chalk slogans and testimonials about mental illness; although these were intended to be gently provocative, they quickly escalated into expressions of night black humor and simmering rage. My favorite among my own contributions was a giant smiley face easily twenty feet in diameter, drawn up like Heath Ledger's Joker from *The Dark Knight*, WHY SO SERIOUS scrawled underneath. I imagine we confused and irritated more people than we inspired, but it was fun. For what it's worth, that weekend I overheard people talking about the chalkings, and a particularly drunk conversant remarked, "Yeah, man, it's like the words of the prophets are written on the subway walls." So something got through to someone, and if I'm uncertain exactly what that was, that's still as much as most student activists accomplish.

My family got along fine, even without me at home vacuuming up all available carbohydrates. My sister began her first semester of college late that August. Both of their children away from home, my parents rededicated themselves to their marriage and their careers. It also was around then that Bear died. He had been faltering for more than a year, growing thinner and frailer. But my dad loved that dog, and the dog loved my father, and neither was willing to let go. Neither the treatment nor the medication seemed to help, and he was obviously in tremendous pain. We put him to sleep late in the summer. We each mourned his passing, the wonderful idiot, none more so than my father. I remain grateful to Bear for his simple devotion in the months surrounding my hospitalization. The house seemed emptier without him. The new quiet was sort of a relief after long months of his sporadic barking, but before that it was undeniably an absence.

It was also around this time that I started to write seriously again. While at the OCDI, I had decided that I wanted to publish for Swarthmore an account of my experiences with the disorder. My initial inspiration was simple enough: I wanted to impress girls. Girls like guys who are funny. Girls like guys with issues: "Baby, I want to be the one you want to fix." With the noblest of intentions, over the following months I took sporadic notes on my personal history of mental illness. My parents and my psychologists, while supportive of this attempt to process my experiences, were uncertain about publication. They quite rightly questioned my motivations and observed that I might invite further trouble by airing my dirty straitjacket so proudly and publicly. By this point, however, the project was already beginning to take shape, and I was hell-bent on bringing it to completion. They sighed collectively, and braced themselves for catastrophe.

As it happened, sadly, my painfully intimate account of personal psychosis brought neither exile nor legions of fawning admirers. The spring of my senior year, I finally published an early version of this memoir in the Swarthmore *Phoenix*. I used an embarrassingly pretentious pseudonym—"Hamlet Wrenncroft" was the only good anagram I found for my name aside from "Flat-worm Entrench"—but other than this I did nothing to conceal my identity. The column triggered a maelstrom of reasoned, respectful critique and broad indifference. I was a little disappointed at first, but while the rewards of publishing were less tangible than controversy or psychosis groupies, I eventually discovered that they were no less gratifying. After a lifetime of absolute social anxiety, of hidden crushes and endless self-recrimination, I let everyone understand exactly what had happened to me and judge me accordingly. I became terribly vulnerable, and in that same instant I became invincible. It would be delusional to assume that everyone had read the columns, of course, but that didn't matter. Whether or not anyone was listening I allowed myself to speak. Freed of the need to hide my illness, in class I went off on lengthy, tenuous explanations of how my experiences with OCD related to Zen Buddhism and Soviet-era Russian speculative fiction. I would not shut up about madness, and although I regret subjecting my friends to anecdotes about suicide at parties, I can't deny how liberating it was.

It ended, inevitably. The spring of my senior year was mostly uneventful, although given my point of comparison I am grateful for this. I sleepwalked an exam or two, and I did my best to support my friends as they struggled through honors-level projects, and then it was done. The day of graduation was gorgeous. My parents and sister were there, of course, as were my aunt and uncle and my two little cousins, and my current girlfriend and several of my friends from the comedy troupe. The speeches were lengthy and of debatable relevance. I found the president's address, his last before his retirement, to be jaw-dropping, sycophantic, and infuriating. Beyond the necessary appeal to alumni donors, it struck me as a cheap lionization of the impulse toward guilty accomplishment, of achievement through self-destruction. "It heightens their resolve to seek excellence defined in increasingly demanding terms. . . . What a vision of undergraduate education Swarthmore projects and delivers. . . . " "Draw on what has proved so effective here!" he advised us, and I thought to myself, No, no, I will not be doing this at all, you scoundrel. The address struck me as a perfect encapsulation of everything poisonous in the institution, of everything that had driven me to madness. But then I was shoved onstage and handed a bit of paper, and then everyone tossed their hats in the air. And that was that.

So one way or another I survived those last few semesters. I wrote and read, I botched exams. I asked a girl for a date in the cafeteria, and we went out for a bit. I completed my thesis while sleeping ten hours a day, and I launched into an irrational tirade against *Monk* before a bewildered friend at Thursday Pub Night. I did silly, exhausting, reprehensible things, some of which still cause me to wince each time I remember them. In the end I was allowed to be a college student, a little, for a bit. I wish I'd had more time to enjoy it. But what matters is that I left Swarthmore a stronger and happier and saner person than I had been when I'd arrived. I am not certain that the lessons I learned were the ones I was intended to, or that the institution deserves credit for all of them. But I suppose that, really, there isn't much more you can ask of an education.

12

Chrono Trigger

What we are reluctant to touch often seems the very
fabric of our salvation.
—Don DeLillo, *White Noise*

Thus, we turn a death trap into a life journey!
—Jack Kirby, *Mister Miracle #18*

This analogy will probably make very little sense to
those of you who do not play videogames. Therefore I
am going to explain it in unnecessary detail. Please bear
with me.

When I was dating The Girl, when we talked about
science fiction and indie music so that we wouldn't
have to talk about other things, the two of us often came
back to one particular video game. It was a role-playing
game for the Super Nintendo called Chrono Trigger.
Although released in the mid-nineties, it still has a great

deal to recommend it: clever design and intricate graphics, dinosaurs, robots, giant monsters. High adventure etc. Its design influenced countless subsequent titles, and one of its most innovative features was intended to increase the game's longevity after the initial playthrough. After you beat the game for the first time—once the apocalyptic beast has become the armored colossus has become the hermaphroditic invertebrate world eater; once you have murdered each of these forms in succession; once the hero gets the girl and the girl gets the throne and the amusing side characters all get closure; and once the credits roll by in series of unpronounceable Japanese names; once all of these things have happened, as they must—a new option will appear on the "Press Start" menu.

Here the player is invited to begin the "New Game Plus." If the option is selected the game begins again exactly as it did the last time. But the catch is that the hero, and each of his companions, is as powerful as he was at the end of last go-around. He hops out of his bed not a defenseless hick, but the level-99 god-killing badass he was when you beat the final boss. The wizard is not an inexperienced punk with little colorful farts of elemental magic but a demon-summoning atomic powerhouse who drops meteors at whim. The girl is not left sticking bandages on her fallen companions but is now able to cure the afflicted and resurrect the dead with a shrug. Entire armies are obliterated before you, incinerated by falling stars or eviscerated by one-hit 9999-point slashes from your ersatz Excalibur. Today it is convention that, once you have beaten a game, you should be allowed to start again with your powers intact. The appeal is no longer the novelty of the game scenarios, but the satisfaction of using your experience and your enhanced characters to breeze past obstacles that once challenged you. It is like reading a book for the second time, only somehow using your foreknowledge of the plot to win a better ending.

It is probably symptomatic of my fascination with videogames that, as I worked on this book, I found myself considering how much more pleasant college would be if I could only restart, somehow begin a new save file with wisdom and experience intact. I imagine marching confidently to the registrar on my first day of registration, a shiny certificate declaring me insane and releasing me forever from the tyranny of deadlines. I imagine being able to enjoy parties without guilt, free of my need to atone through sporadic periods of self-recrimination and half-assed asceticism. I imagine approaching girls with absolute competence, accepting their scathing rejection with Zen detachment. I imagine taking courses and writing on my own, free to express myself without the interference of the disorder. I imagine spending time with my friends, finally able to enjoy those afternoons and evenings poisoned by madness, once lost.

As I write this it has been about a year since my graduation. The events immediately following the ceremony were a flurry of gowns and flowers and the whirring of digital cameras. Within a few hours we bade farewell to my aunt and uncle and little cousins, and escorted my sister to her flight back to Chicago. I said good-bye to my girlfriend. My mother and father and I piled everything into the car and we left Swarthmore College, together, for the last time.

When I returned home I was greeted by Moonbeam, who bounded over to the door and flopped down on his back next to my bag, demanding that I rub his belly. He seemed thin, haggard. My mother told me that he had been eating less and less over the past few months, and we immediately made an appointment with his veterinarian. He had anemia and bone cancer. It was incurable. Surgery would be painful and expensive and could not have given him more than a few months. In the last few days of his life we let Moonbeam run free, outside, the way he wanted to when he was younger. On the Thursday after I graduated we had him euthanized. That is an ugly word, and I understand that "put to sleep" is gentler, but the decision we made was ugly and painful and I cannot bring myself to soften it in print. I always thought that he would pass away some night, quietly, in his sleep. I thought the little bastard would live forever.

I think it's always difficult to explain the connection one feels with a pet, especially in writing. Even if you are an animal lover, even if you have lost one of your own, it is difficult to do anything more than nod sympathetically at the death of a stranger's animal. Something essential, what made the animal special, is often lost. Bear and Moony were wonderful, unique animals. More so than any human, including my family and myself, they intuitively understood how I suffered and did everything in their power to comfort me. In their own way, each of them fought as hard as I did to keep me alive and sane. Since I am not eloquent enough to convey the full strength of their personalities, consider instead what they taught me. Bear was being; Bear was acceptance. Bear was utter unself-conscious presence, the joyful pursuit of the moment so absolute that he would crash into a tree chasing it. And Moony: Moony was perversity. Moony was "no." Moony was spiteful and nasty and wicked, Moony would fight with every aspect of his being against any restriction, against any wall or lock or door. Acceptance and perversity. They showed me, every day, everything I needed to overcome the disorder, and although I did not recognize this they attended to me nonetheless. My loyal, dumb Caliban and my obese Ariel. I don't think I will ever stop missing them.

While writing this memoir I returned to Philadelphia. Hoping to remain in touch with my friends from school, I found an apartment in the Swarthmore Ville. This decision came with no small amount of anxiety, as I was convinced that staying so close to the school demonstrated that I was a creepy, irredeemable loser and that I had proved myself unable to function outside of college. Over time, however, I decided that I was expecting too much of myself. Sometimes, I have determined, it's okay to be a little bit of a loser. We do what we need to do to get by. And with significant support from my family I have made faltering, tentative steps toward independent adulthood. I've worked part-time as a tutor. I have kept up with my friends from college and probably spent as much time enjoying their company over these past months as I did over my four years in school. Some of us formed a new comedy group, and we've done a few shows in Philadelphia. I continued treatment for my OCD with Sal, who now practices in a swanky Rittenhouse Square office in Philadelphia. My girlfriend stayed with me for a few more months and then I got dumped on my ass; she originally told me that she didn't have time for a relationship because of her classes at Swarthmore, although later she complained that she was overwhelmed by persistent, nagging doubts as to whether her feelings for me were genuine. In light of this reasoning, I entertain the possibility that our split was for the best. In any case, as unpleasant as that was, when I compare it to my previous significant breakup I cannot help but be grateful for how much has changed.

And I have written this. It would be nice to claim that when I look back at the neurotic, misguided little scamp I was at eighteen, I hardly recognize him, but that would be a lie. I recognize him perfectly. He is me, but me crippled, mutilated, and broken so thoroughly he is unaware of the fracture. I see myself chained and shackled, a bony emaciated ghost, clutching blind at the lattice of the disorder. It would be inappropriate to say that I feel sorry for myself now, because I don't, but I feel sorry for him. For them. I feel tremendously sorry for them. The young man, clenched and sobbing, trying not to tear himself apart; the dull and sullen adolescent, sneering and hypocritical, his most corrosive venom held in reserve for himself; the bright child with the troubled eyes; the little boy sprawled on the floor among cheap plastic toys, trying and failing to build a world that makes sense. They hurt. They hurt still, somewhere within me.

Yet there is nothing I can do for them. My childhood, my adolescence, my college years: They are gone. They were mutilated into something unbearable, and that I experienced fleeting moments of quiet and contentment through that nightmare mesh I owe to my friends and loved ones. Even now, there is not a single happy memory I can conjure up that does not bring other memories of neurosis and sickness and terror. But the old selves, the young man and the boys, are gone. I cannot save them or reverse their pain. All I can do is live my own life now, as best I can; and remember, with respect and sympathy, their trials and their mistakes; and hope that, from the ruins of their suffering, I can build something worthwhile.

I hope I have made something worthwhile, here. I know it has been useful for me, drawing out and dissecting every instance of illness since my early childhood, but I also hope it has been worthwhile for you. I understand that my symptoms are unusual in their severity, but please do not let this create some artificial wall between us. If there is some lesson you can take from my story, please do so.

I have spent much of my time since my diagnosis considering the plight of the mentally ill in contemporary society. I have come to think of us as a minority of sorts, although one without precedent. We are united not by distinction, but by a burden that any of us would shed gleefully. We chuckle and cringe in the face of colossal ignorance, in a society that mocks us, or condemns us, or flatly refuses to acknowledge that we exist. We suffer alone, and pointlessly, and in silence. Our power is not in that which makes us different but in the strength we muster to overcome these differences and conform, to live

unremarkable lives while hiding exquisite personal torture. Every day survived under such conditions is an en-
deavor and an achievement. Every B is a victory.

Since childhood I have been reassured that we are all
human, that everyone is the same on the inside. I wonder,
where does that leave people like me, who are demonstrably not the same on the inside? We are misunderstood
mutants like the X-Men, only not the cool, popular
X-Men; we are like Marrow, whose face was disfigured
by bony protrusions, or like Maggott, whose digestive
system was replaced by a pair of intelligent armored slugs.
I am *Homo obsessus:* literally "besieged man." My brain,
my mind, my soul—whatever terrestrial or transcenden-
tal organ you choose to assign responsibility for the
functionality of my person—does not work. It is broken,
and it has consequently spent the duration of its existence
trying to dismantle itself. My better angel is defective,
and the manufacturer has been extremely uncooperative
in my attempts to obtain a replacement. Indeed, much of
my treatment has involved convincing myself not to approach the executive prematurely, to demand an explanation of his organization's incompetence.

So to anyone reading who also struggles with mental
illness: I am sorry. I am so sorry. I am sorry for what you
have been through, and I am sorry that no one, certainly
not I, can understand the unique nature of your suffering. If I could give you advice: Learn to lay your burden

down, if you can. Do what you have to so that you can heal. It may help you to talk about what you have endured; it helped me. Does it sound embarrassing, trite, if I claim that I feel a kinship between us? I don't care. I don't care at all anymore. You are my brother, my sister.

Now for the rest of you bastards. I understand my story may have less immediate relevance to you, with your wonderful shiny brains squirting around all those healthy neurochemicals. But please consider: Obsession is not limited to those afflicted by OCD. I believe that everyone has this tendency to think in circles, trying to neutralize what we cannot control. We lock ourselves up, hoping to protect against the inevitable. We write rules and laws, we draw arbitrary comparisons. We make judgments. We skirt past the unfamiliar alleyways and hold our breath past the graveyards. We do all of these things to protect ourselves from the absolute terror of pure being, and yet they accomplish nothing. The Hindus call it *ahimsa:* attachment. Supposedly when you rid yourself of it, you achieve Buddhahood and ascend to a higher level of existence. I haven't seen that happen yet. I promise if I do I'll let you know.

So if I have advice for you it is this. Imagine the worst thing in the world. Think the unthinkable. Find the hidden places where you refuse to trespass, those principles that you have sworn never to break; and then start to consider what, perhaps, might happen to you if you broke them. Recognize when you are afraid and learn when you cannot protect yourself. Learn to accept horrible and inevitable things. Learn to be heartbroken, to be hopeless, and then to get better. Understand that, although it may be painful, you can never not profit when you learn something about yourself. Do terrifying things. Live. Fucking live. I mean that.

So this is it, this is the end of the proverbial session. Writing this has been a long, ugly, difficult process, just as my past four years have been long, ugly, and difficult years. I've made mistakes and I've contradicted myself, but I do not regret writing or publishing this. The narrative does not stop, things accelerate, and everything will change soon again. Imagine life as Russian roulette, played using a revolver with infinite empty chambers, loaded with a single bullet. Imagine someone is pointing a gun at your head, and every breath is another spinning cylinder, and every heartbeat is another strike of the hammer. Only now, after twenty-three years of terrifying and anticlimactic clicks, have I begun to understand this. One day I will be unlucky, one day the bullet will align with the barrel and nothing I can do will stop it: There will be a sound as large as the world, interrupted, and then annihilating white. And I'll be gone. But hell, I've been lucky so far, right? I feel the muzzle cold at my temple and I squeeze my eyes tight, I smile. I pull the trigger. I'm still breathing.

CPSIA information can be obtained at www.ICGtesting.com
Printed in the USA
LVOW11*1823150615

442547LV00005B/26/P

9 780312 622107